Language in early childhood education

Contributors

Joan C. Baratz
Director
Education Policy Institute
300-1800 Massachusetts
    Avenue, N.W.
Washington, DC 20036

Elsa J. Bartlett
Assistant Professor
Neurology Department
New York University Medical
    Center
530 First Avenue
New York, NY 10016

Betty H. Bryant
Senior Curriculum Advisor
Early Education
Boston School Department
26 Court Street
Boston, MA 02108

Courtney B. Cazden
Professor of Education
Harvard Graduate School of
    Education
Longfellow Hall, Room 205
13 Appian Way
Cambridge, MA 02138

Carol Chomsky
Lecturer in Education
Harvard Graduate School of
    Education
Larson Hall, Room 207
Appian Way
Cambridge, MA 02138

Jean Berko Gleason
Professor of Psychology
Boston University
Department of Psychology
64 Cummington Street
Boston, MA 02215

Janet Gonzalez-Mena
Instructor
Solano Community College
Suisun Valley Road
Suisun, CA 94585

William Labov
Professor of Linguistics and
    Psychology
University of Pennsylvania
Philadelphia, PA 19174

Ilse Mattick
Coordinator
Therapeutic Tutoring Program
Associate Professor of Early
    Childhood Education and
    Psychology
Wheelock College
Boston, MA 02215

Francis H. Palmer
Visiting Professor
University of California-
    Los Angeles
Los Angeles, CA 90024

Melissa Tillman
Director of Educational Services
Action for Boston Community
    Development
City Hall
Boston, MA 02111

Barbara Tizard
Reader in Education
Thomas Coram Research Unit
University of London Institute of
    Education
41 Brunswick Square
London WC1N 1AZ

Language in early childhood education

revised edition
Courtney B. Cazden, Editor

National Association for the Education of Young Children
Washington, D.C.

Cover art:
Drawing—Alberto Hernandez. *The Harvard Gradutae School of Education Association Bulletin,* Spring/Summer 1975.
Design—Rebecca J. Miller

Photographs:
Alan Borrud 79
Faith Bowlus 89
Carvis Bullock 103
Paul S. Conklin 23
Sandy Felsenthal 137
Sally Gale 131
Marietta Lynch 112
Lois Main 84
Susan Pavane 93
Diane Pierce 143
Rick Reinhard 126
Stephen H. Saperstone 2
Michael Schulman 6
Michael D. Sullivan 154
Elaine M. Ward 147

Copyright © 1981. All rights reserved.
Reprinted January 1987, October 1989.
National Association for the Education of Young Children
1834 Connecticut Ave., N.W.
Washington, DC 20009

Library of Congress Catalog Card Number: 81-82158
ISBN Catalog Number: 0-912674-74-1
NAEYC #131

Printed in the United States of America

In Memoriam

This book is dedicated to the memory of three very special friends of young children who died of cancer in the summer of 1979 as the final writing was done.

Dorothy Cohen, Senior Faculty Member of the Bank Street College of Education, New York City

Wendy Simon, day care teacher in Greenfield, Massachusetts and the United Farm Workers day care center in La Paz, California

Jack Tizard, Research Professor of Child Development, Thomas Coram Research Unit, Institute of Education, London

Contents

Preface

This is a revised edition of *Language in Early Childhood Education,* which was originally published in 1972. The first edition has been on the best-selling list of NAEYC books each year. I hope this revised edition will be as successful.

For those familiar with the first edition, there are several major changes: Elsa Bartlett has updated her consumer's guide to published language curricula, including materials available through 1978. From London, Barbara Tizard reports on her comparative research analyzing language at home and at school. Because ideas from Great Britain are now included in Bartlett's review and Tizard's chapter, my outdated report on language programs in England and Wales has been deleted. Janet Gonzalez-Mena's article on English as a second language has been added; and I have rewritten the introductory chapters in each section.

In these chapters, terms such as *center, program,* and *preschool* are used interchangeably, as are *teacher* and *caregiver.* However, there is an important distinction—whatever terms may be used—between ideas for language curricula (see especially Chapters 4, 5, 10, and 11) that are useful at particular places and times in the preschool day, and general characteristics of the full-day child care environment that are important for language development. These characteristics are discussed in the first section and in Chapters 6 and 8.

Each chapter has its own list of references. Entries marked with an asterisk are included in Appendix A.

As with the first edition, this revision was made possible by the support of the Ford Foundation and its Program Officer, Marjorie Martus. Final work on the revision was completed while I was a Fellow at the Center for Advanced Study in the Behavioral Sciences. Support from the National Endowment for the Humanities and the Spencer Foundation is gratefully acknowledged.

Courtney B. Cazden

Part I
Early Language Experiences

It is important both to provide settings in which the children feel comfortable and at home, and to help them learn new styles of talking expected in school.

Courtney B. Cazden

1.
Language Development and the Preschool Environment

Planning preschool and day care environments to support children's language development is a means of augmenting language development at home. I will describe briefly what we know about early language acquisition. DeVilliers and deVilliers (1979) and Weeks (1979) provide more detailed accounts of this subject. I also discuss the unique aspects of the school setting that have to be considered when examining early acquisition. I conclude the chapter with two postscripts that I feel are well-worth remembering. In Chapter 2, Tizard continues the discussion of language at home and at school through a more direct comparison.

Early language development

When we say that children have learned their native language by the time they enter first grade, what do we mean they have learned? A set of sentences from which they choose the appropriate one when they want to say something? The meaning of a set of sentences from which they choose the correct interpretation for the sentence they hear? Even if they are able to interpret numerous sentences and meanings, their ability would still be inadequate. Other than a few greetings such as "Good morning" and clichés such as "My, it's hot today," few sentences are repeatedly spoken or heard. Any speaker, child or adult, is continuously saying and comprehending sentences she or he has never heard before and will never hear nor comprehend again in the same way. Creativity in expressing and understanding particular meanings in particular settings to and from particular listeners is the core of all human language ability.

A more accurate explanation for what we call "knowing a language" is that children learn a limited set of rules. Of course we do not mean that they know the rules in any conscious way. The rules are assimilated non-consciously, as a kind of tacit knowledge. This way of knowing occurs in adults too. Few of us can state the rules for adding /s/, /z/, or /iz/ sounds to form plural nouns. Yet if asked to supply the plural endings for nonsense words such as *bik, wug,* or *gutch* (Berko 1958), all native speakers of English could easily do so. Most six-year-old children can too. We infer knowledge of language rules from what adults or children can say and understand.

Children learn their native language gradually. Might one assume, therefore, that the stages they pass through on their way to mature knowledge could be characterized as partial versions of adult knowledge? Not so! One of the most dramatic findings of studies of child language acquisition is that these stages show striking similarities across children but equally striking deviations from the adult system.

For example, while children are learning to form noun and verb endings, at a certain period in their development they say *foots* instead of *feet, goed* instead of *went, mines* instead of *mine* (Cazden 1972). Children do not hear *foots* or *goed* or *mines.* These words are overgeneralizations of rules that children somehow extract from the language they do hear. Children hear *hers, his, ours, yours,* and *theirs;* and they hypothesize that the first-person singular should be *mines.* Human beings are pattern- or rule-discovering animals, and these incorrect generalizations of tacitly discovered rules for the formation of words are actively constructed in children's minds as an oversimplification of the structure of the language they hear.

Rules for formation of sentences show the same kinds of deviations. In learning how to ask a question, children will say, "Why I can't go?," neglecting temporarily to reverse the auxiliary *can't* and pronoun *I.* Their answer to the often-asked question, "What are you doing?," will temporarily be, "I am doing dancing." If the answer to "What are you eating?" assumes the form "I am eating X," children hypothesize that the answer to "What are you doing?" is, "I am doing X-ing." Only later do they learn that answers with *doing* require the exceptional form "I am X-ing."

Sometimes we get even more dramatic evidence of how impervious to external alteration the child's rule system can be. Gleason's reported conversation with a four-year-old is an example:

> She said, "My teacher holded the baby rabbits and we patted them."
> I asked, "Did you say your teacher held the baby rabbits?"
> She answered, "Yes."
> I then asked, "What did you say she did?"
> She answered, again. "She holded the baby rabbits and we patted them."
> "Did you say she held them tightly?" I asked.
> "No," she answered, "she holded them loosely." (Gleason 1967, p. 1)

When parents try deliberately to teach children a form that does not fit their present rule system, the same filtering process occurs. The following conversation took place when a psychologist tried to correct an immaturity in her daughter's speech:

C. "Nobody don't like me."
M. "No, say 'Nobody likes me.' "
C. "Nobody don't like me."
  (eight repetitions of this dialogue)
M. *"No. Now listen carefully; say 'Nobody likes me.' "*
C. *"Oh! Nobody don't likes me."* (McNeill 1966, p. 69)

Irregular verbs such as *went* and *came* are some of the most common verbs in English. Children usually learn the irregular forms first, evidently as isolated vocabulary words, and later start constructing their own over-generalizations *goed* and *comed* when they reach the stage of tacitly discovering that particular rule. Finally, they achieve the mature pattern of rule plus exceptions. Stages on the way to the child's acquisition of mature behavior may for the moment resemble regressions, as errors in terms of adult standards. However, these stages are significant evidence of intellectual work and linguistic progress.

With a very few pathological exceptions, all children learn to speak the language of their parents and home community. They do so with such speed and ease, at an age when other seemingly simpler learnings such as identification of colors are absent, that one wonders how this process is accomplished, and what role environment plays. Here we can contrast research with common myths.

Myth 1: Children learn language by imitation. The commonsense view of how children learn to speak is that they imitate the language they hear. In a general way, this must be true. Children in an English-speaking home speak English, not French or some language of their own. But a close examination of the language learning process reveals that all of a child's skills are not due to imitation. As *foots,* and *goes,* and *holded* show, children use the language they hear as examples of language to learn from, not samples of language to learn.

While imitation is not as important as commonly believed, identification with particular models is very important. How people speak depends not only on who they are, but on how they see themselves in relation to others, on who they want to be. From the beginning of the language learning process, children pick their models. This is not done consciously, but we have already observed the power of nonconscious knowledge. If children did not pick their models, there would be no way to explain why Black children, for example, speak like their parents or peers despite considerable exposure to standard English on television. Attitudes about language greatly influence the learning process and they must be taken into consideration. They influence teachers' responses to children as well as children's responses to teachers.

Language is learned not because we want to talk about language, but because we want to talk about the world.

Myth 2: Children learn language by being corrected. Just as the commonsense view holds that the child's language learning process is basically through imitation, so it asserts that the adult's contribution is to shape children's speech by correcting them when they are wrong and reinforcing them when they are correct. This is another false assumption. All analyses of conversations between parents and children whose language is developing clearly show that neither correction of immature forms nor reinforcement of mature forms occurs with sufficient frequency to be a potent force.

During conversations with their children, parents do correct misstatements of fact (such as when a particular television program is scheduled); parents provide labels and clarify word meanings (for example, the difference between *beside* and *under*); parents correct language they consider socially inappropriate; and they directly teach socially important routines such as "bye-bye" and "thank you" (Gleason and Weintraub 1976). Perhaps most important of all, parents speak to young children with simpler language than when adults are addressed. As the child's utterances become longer and more complex, so do the parents' (Snow and Ferguson 1977). Other than this simplification, there is no sequencing of what children have to learn. They are offered a cafeteria, not a carefully prescribed diet. Seemingly impelled from within, children participate in the give-and-take of conversation as best they can from the very beginning, and in the process take what they need to build their own language system.

This picture of how children learn their native language *before* school is fairly clear, but implications for how best to help children continue their learning *in* school are far less certain. The most obvious implication is that teachers should act the way parents have acted: talk with children about topics of mutual interest in the context of ongoing work and play. But our planning for language development has to go further than that if we are to meet all the needs of all children.

Children in school need varying kinds and amounts of help, and it is important not to waste time and attention where help is not needed. For example, some programs such as DISTAR (described in Chapter 4) require children to practice making negative statements such as "That is not a pen." Because it seemed likely that four-year-olds could use these negative structures in their spontaneous speech, a research assistant, Tina Schrager, spent many hours in a Head Start program which used a DISTAR-like program, recording children's negative statements in all situations except the language lesson itself. She worked out a set of structural categories, and she remained at work (for 14-16 hours in each of the three groups) until she had examples of all but the most complex from all the children, even those in their first term in this program. Figure 1.1 gives utterances in all four structural categories for three of these recently enrolled children.

These data do not mean that language education is not needed. For example, these children may need practice in certain cognitive tasks which require the comprehension of negative statements such as "Draw something that is not a circle." Here they would have to avoid drawing the shape actually mentioned and respond to the *not* by bringing to mind, and thence to paper, something which has not been said. This is a far harder cognitive task than simply making negative statements about visible objects.

Areas in which children need help may not always be obvious. Gerald was a 33-month-old child from a low-income Black family who attended a day care center in the Boston community of Roxbury. In language structure, his development was remarkably advanced. Here are the 7 longest utterances recorded in a play session with an adult before Gerald was 3 years old:

"I'm looking for a cup.
I waiting for a other cup.
You put it up on there like dis.
I gon' put dis one in 'nere.
Look at what I made with dis one.
Den gon' put dis one back in here cause it fell out.
I'm gonna knock dese things in.
Soon I get finish I gon' do dat way.
Can I take it off and put it on?" (Cazden 1972, p. 187)

Figure 1.1: Negative Utterances from Three Children

	Negative and imperative	Negative and main verb	Negative and auxiliary	Negative and indefinite
Darnell	Don't take all of it.	My name ain't Gail. You don't know how.	No, you can't do 3's. Why can't we pull this up? I can't either. You can't do like this.	We don't have nothing to cut with. I don't want any cheese.
Laura	Not over here, over there.	You don't have no badge on. I don't like green peppers. I don't like J. I don't like Mom. That 8's not upside down.	You can't do it. I can't do this. We can't dig it 'cause snow's on the ground. I can't hear you. I can't see you. I'm not gonna do it on the back. I'm not gonna fall. That girl don't supposed to have no dress on a rainy day.	I never seen green.

Aaron			
Don't do that.	No, this 3 is not lying down.	Lester won't stop.	I never taste that.
Don't mess up my thing.	This string is not straight.	You can't play.	Don't put no little ones there.
Don't mess up that.	I didn't.	Paul won't stop.	
	We didn't talk about that, right?		
Don't take them.	We don't eat it.		
Don't put no little ones there.	I don't eat green peppers.		
	No, we didn't.		
	My mother don't cook that.		
Don't bend it.	I don't like green peas.		
	We don't have them.		
	Not me.		
	He don't do his 8's right.		
	Them are not 8's.		
	That's not a 8.		
	That's not a white triangle.		
	You don't like it like this?		
	No, I don't want to.		

These are all well-formed utterances, one with 12 words! But perhaps what is not obvious is that all these sentences will only be meaningful when Gerald and the person he is talking to share an immediately present context. He may need help with the kinds of referential tasks described in Chapter 5, and maybe with vocabulary building too.

In order to ensure that Gerald obtains such help, and that other children have their needs met, we have to consider the structure of the school environment itself.

The structure of the school environment

One decision about the language program which preschool teachers must make is to what extent encounters should be preplanned with children, and how much they can rely on responding or initiating spontaneously as they watch and listen to the children at work and at play. This is one component of structure in the preschool. Mayer (1971) points out that there is a structure to all aspects of any preschool environment. Certain materials are chosen and placed in certain locations; others are omitted. Activities are arranged: some that children can carry out alone, like painting a picture; others that require at least two children to play together, like riding a seesaw; still others that require the guidance of an adult, like cooking. We are concerned here only with the structure of conversations—among children, or between them and any adult. The important question is how to plan for these conversations so that children's language development is nurtured more than if the children were simply left to play and talk with whomever appeared on the street or playground.

First, *we have to consider not just the overall preschool environment, but the environment of each individual child.* One aspect of any group setting is that teachers must distribute their attention and their conversational time among all of the children. Complicating this distribution is the impossibility of devoting equal time to each child. A group environment can be 24 different environments for 24 children. Because teachers themselves respond to reinforcement, they may talk more to the children who talk most to them. In other words, how individual children talk (or do not talk) affects the teacher's behavior and distribution of conversational time.

Monaghan (1971) researched this problem in a Cambridge nursery school which has a child group mixed in age, race, and social class. Ignoring these differences, Monaghan kept a record of who initiated conversations and then compared the list of children ranked according to the number of verbal contacts they initiated with any teacher to the list of the same children ranked according to the number of verbal contacts any teacher initiated with them. The two lists were very similar, and more so in the spring than in the fall. Monaghan stated that over the course of the year,

> The teaching staff appears to be reinforcing and amplifying what already exists when children enter—those children who initiate a great deal get teacher initiations in return, while those who initiate infrequently are not frequently

sought out by teachers. By omission or commission, the general configuration of social abilities or deficits which a child brings with him to school will be strengthened as classroom policy now stands. (1971, p. 17)

A preschool environmental structure should be developed that will guarantee a more equal distribution of teacher attention by setting certain times for a teacher and a small group of children to talk together, so that conversation is not solely dependent on child initiative in using adults as a resource for help and information. Chapter 4 describes many curricula that can be used during such small group periods.

Second, *children come to school with experiences in certain kinds of conversation settings and with their own preferred ways of relating verbally or nonverbally to others.* Cazden, John, and Hymes (1972) give many examples of cultural differences in these preferences. Featherstone (1974) uncovered some intriguing facts about the settings in which children chose to spend their time in the same Cambridge nursery school where Monaghan observed. A kitchen was available as one setting for the children. Featherstone noticed that in 25 observations in the kitchen, certain children were there very often while others were rarely present. What was special about the kitchen? Not eating, as little tasting was done. She suggests that activity in the kitchen had several characteristics. It was the only place in the school that always had a stationary adult, and it had an activity structured in two ways: by teacher direction, telling children what to do to help prepare the day's recipe; and by a definite beginning, middle, and end to the activity itself. In further observations, Featherstone found that the children most often in the kitchen were also most often found in the other school setting, an art room, where an adult was sometimes stationary. These same children sought out the occasional stationary adult in other settings of the school more than their peers did. It is important both to provide settings in which the children feel comfortable and at home, and to help them learn new styles of talking expected in school.

Third, *conversations with young children will be richer in content if there is continuity and consistency in the adult-child relationship.* Teachers are inevitably less familiar with their students than the individual child's parents. Mothers and fathers may be superb conversationalists for their young children not only because of the powerful affective climate which enhances the child's attention, but also because they know the child and her or his world so well. When children in their second year of life can utter only a few meaningful words, a mother and father are most likely to understand the child's idiosyncratic pronunciation and will be able to make a meaningful response. If the child says, "Baa," the parent can respond, "Your blanket? It's in the kitchen, on your chair," whereas no one outside the family would understand. Later, when the child's speech more closely approximates normal pronunciation and is therefore intelligible to a wider audience, idiosyncrasies will remain, and the child will speak egocentrically in the sense of assuming that the listener knows the referents for the child's words. When a boy not yet three years old announced "Betty and I played radio last night," his father understood that Betty Bryant, a graduate student, had been there with her tape recorder; but only the three-year-old's mother knew that Betty had actually come earlier that day rather than the previous night, and so only she could correct the child's expression of past time. Someone less intimately involved with the family could have said little more than, "Oh, that's nice," while wondering about the boy's activities. Margaret Mead (1973) uses her own experience as a grandmother to speak of the importance of a shared world:

> I was walking along a Cambridge street with my two-year-old granddaughter and we stopped in front of a florist shop. She stared in the window and said, "Never be a cat." What would you say? Most grandmothers would say, "Yes, dearie, see that nice doggie," but I knew what she was talking about. Because I knew she was referring to a song that my grandmother sang to me, that I sang to my daughter, that my daughter sang to her, which said, "Always be a pussy, never be a cat. / They call me pussywillow, and what do you think of that?" There was a pussywillow in the florist window. Now, this is what our children don't have and this is what we have to begin to put together for them. This is the reason for bringing parents into the child care center and into the nursery school. It is a reason for bringing the teachers into the homes of the children. It is an attempt to establish at least a certain degree of commonality so that people can talk to each other and have some identity. (1973, p. 327)

In preschools and child care centers children speak to adults (or peers) who are unfamiliar with their language and world. The problem is magnified for children younger than three years old. It is also magnified in all-day care: children encounter a larger set of adults each week (changing shifts of staff, different volunteers each day, etc.), and it is in this group environment children spend the majority of the speaking day. Under these conditions, unless teachers talk frequently with parents, visit children at home, and get to know a few children really well, meaningful extended conversation will necessarily be more limited. Consistency in adult-child relationships may be as important for language as for affective development during the early years (even though an opposite case can be made for the beneficial challenge to older children of communicating with strangers). This consistency with young children may be more frequent in programs where teachers are assigned to work and talk with specific small groups for part of each day.

Finally, *there is the ever-present danger of overemphasizing children's "errors," and spending too much time on problems of control.* Partly this danger is a matter of attitude. Suppose that while looking at a picture, a child says, "He fall down." Consider the following alternative responses: *Expansion:* "Yes, he fell *down.*" *Correction:* "No, he *fell* down." The warm, confirming quality of the expansion contrasts with the critical and impatient manner of the correction. The expansion, in substance and tone, focuses on how much the child has already achieved, while still indicating the direction for further growth; the correction stresses the gap still remaining between the child's point in language development and the projected goals. While parents are more apt to speak from care and confidence, I am afraid **teachers are more** apt to speak in a negative and corrective tone. (Schachter's [1979] discussion on how to talk with young children emphasizes the relationship between affective and cognitive development.)

In addition to the influence of a teacher's attitude, *organization* is also important. When life at school is hectic, teacher talk will be more managerial than informative, and such talk invites silence, not dialogue. Moreover, conversations that do get started will be cut short by noise and interruptions. That may be one reason why the first and most important finding of the National Day Care Study (Ruopp 1979) is that group size, even more than caregiver/child ratio, is an important influence on the quality of care:

> Across all study sites, smaller groups are consistently associated with better care, more socially active children and higher gains on two developmental tests. (Ruopp 1979, p. 2)

Thus, two adults for 14 children would be better than three adults for 21 children, even though the caregiver/child ratio remains the same. This fits also with the findings of Tizard, Cooperman, Joseph, and Tizard (1972) on the organizational conditions in residential nurseries in England that promote informative rather than managerial talk, discussed in Chapter 8.

Two postscripts

This entire book is about language and I would like to add two special postscripts that must be remembered. *Words are only one form of creative expression.* Young children can express and transform experiences and ideas through blocks, paints, clay, and movement, as well as words. Graves (n.d.) found in his study of young children's writing in the primary grades that "in environments where the *only* form of expression is in writing, writing suffers." The same is surely true of talking for younger children. So while this book is just about language, in early childhood education language cannot flourish alone.

Having thought about how to plan the school environment so that children's language can develop, I realized that in the same environment language itself has to recede into the background of attention so that *we may hear through the language what we and the children are trying to say.* For ourselves, we can do no better than heed the wise words of Brown (1977). At the end of a long introduction to a book about research on the characteristics of parental speech to young children, he speaks directly to parents and, by extension, to all other caregivers as well:

> Believe that your child can understand more than he or she can say, and seek, above all, to communicate. To understand and be understood. To keep your minds fixed on the same target. In doing that, you will, without thinking about it, make 100 or maybe 1000 alterations in your speech and action. Do not try to practice them as such. There is no set of rules of how to talk to a child that can

even approach what you unconsciously know. If you concentrate on communicating, everything else will follow. (1977, p. 26)

For the children, we must remember that only linguists have language as their subject matter. For the rest of us—especially for children—*language is learned not because we want to talk about language, but because we want to talk about the world.* One of the language programs included in Chapter 4 is actually a book about physical knowledge (Kamii and DeVries 1978), or what might be called science experiences. We are especially glad to include it as an indication of how language can flourish indirectly by careful planning in all curriculum areas.

References

Berko, J. "The Child's Learning of English Morphology." *Word* 14 (1958): 150-177.

Brown, R. "Introduction." In *Talking to Children: Language Input and Acquisition*, eds. C. E. Snow and C. A. Ferguson. New York: Cambridge University Press, 1977.

* Cazden, C. B. *Child Language and Education.* New York: Holt, Rinehart & Winston, 1972.

* Cazden, C. B.; John, V. P.; and Hymes, D., eds. *Functions of Language in the Classroom.* New York: Teachers College Press, 1972.

* deVilliers, P. A., and deVilliers, J. G. *Early Language.* Cambridge, Mass.: Harvard University Press, 1979.

Featherstone, H. "The Use of Settings in a Heterogeneous Preschool." *Young Children* 29, no. 3 (March 1974): 147-154.

Gleason, J. B. "Do Children Imitate?" *Proceedings of the International Conference on Oral Education of the Deaf.* Vol. II (June 1967): 1441-1448.

Gleason, J. B., and Weintraub, S. "The Acquisition of Routines in Child Language: 'Trick or Treat.'" *Language in Society* 5 (1976): 129-136.

Graves, D. H. "Bullock and Beyond: Research on the Writing Process." Unpublished paper, University of New Hampshire, n.d.

Kamii, C., and DeVries, R. *Physical Knowledge in Preschool Education.* Englewood Cliffs, N.J.: Prentice-Hall, 1978.

Mayer, R. S. "A Comparative Analysis of Preschool Curriculum Models." In *Readings in Early Childhood Education*, eds. R. Anderson and H. Shane. Boston: Houghton Mifflin, 1971.

McNeill, D. "Developmental Psycholinguistics." In *The Genesis of Language: A Psycholinguistic Approach*, eds. F. Smith and G. A. Miller. Cambridge, Mass.: MIT Press, 1966.

Mead, M. "Can the Socialization of Children Lead to Greater Acceptance of Diversity?" *Young Children* 28, no. 6 (August 1973): 322-332.

Monaghan, A. C. "Children's Contacts: Some Preliminary Findings." Unpublished term paper, Harvard Graduate School of Education, 1971.

Ruopp, R. *Children at the Center: Final Report of the National Day Care Study.* Washington, D.C.: U.S. Department of Health, Education and Welfare, 1979.

Schachter, F. F. *Everyday Mother Talk to Toddlers: Early Intervention.* New York: Academic Press, 1979.

Snow, C. E., and Ferguson, C. A., eds. *Talking to Children: Language Input and Acquisition.* Cambridge: Cambridge University Press, 1977.

Tizard, B.; Cooperman, O.; Joseph, A.; and Tizard, J. "Environmental Effects on Language Development: A Study of Young Children in Long-Stay Residential Nurseries." *Child Development* 43 (1972): 337-358.

Weeks, T. E. *Born to Talk.* Rowley, Mass.: Newbury House, 1979.

Barbara Tizard

2.
Language at Home and at School

There is a very widespread belief among professionals who deal with young children that the language usage in working-class homes is "inadequate." This inadequacy is often seen as the main cause of early educational difficulties, although what the exact nature of the inadequacy is, and how it causes educational failure, is not usually analyzed. Because of this belief, there is a growing trend to attempt to influence the way in which these parents communicate with their children, either by sending specially trained visitors to their homes, or by encouraging them to attend workshops and other programs. As a preventive measure, it is considered important to enroll working-class children in nursery school, where the skill and knowledge of the teacher can be used to "give measured attention to the children's language needs (Bullock 1975)."

There is certainly good evidence of social-class differences both in childrearing patterns and in children's achievement on standardized tests. What is questionable is the interpretation of these differences and the policy implications drawn from the interpretation. There is, in fact, very little direct evidence available about the way language is used in working-class homes. Naturalistic studies by Wootton (1974) and Wells (1975) suggest that in fact social-class differences in language usage are relatively small.

The popular belief that sending working-class children to nursery school will remove them from an impoverished language environment to a rich one is equally unsubstantiated. I found in recent interviews with nursery school staff that they almost all believed that the working-class children's biggest advantage from school attendance was exposure to enriched language experiences (Tizard 1978). Only 3 out of 142 parents gave this response, however. Almost all saw the gain to the child in social terms—mixing with other children, becoming more independent of mother, etc. Before the study reported here, we could not find any evidence that the

This study was carried out with Helen Carmichael, Martin Hughes, and Gillian Pinkerton.

home and nursery school, as language development environments, had been systematically compared.

One reason for teachers believing that nursery school stimulates language development is that teachers do a lot of talking. In our observation of nursery school teachers we found them talking to the children in 50 percent of the five-second observation periods (Tizard et al. 1976). If, however, one observes the child rather than the staff, then the amount of conversation addressed to each individual child is much more limited because the staff-child ratio in British nursery schools is approximately 1:10.

Still, even this amount of talk could possibly be more than the children were receiving at home. It is also possible that conversations at home are of such poor quality that even a limited amount of superior quality teacher verbal attention could be of benefit to the child. To investigate these possibilities we compared the conversations children had with the staff at school to those they had with their mothers at home.

Half of the 30 girls observed were daughters of working-class parents, the other half were middle-class children. The working-class children in our study could not in any reasonable sense be considered deprived; they lived with their small, two-parent families, the majority in low-cost housing, and they appeared to be well cared for, much loved, and were well supplied with toys. Since nursery schooling in Britain, although free, is not compulsory, it is possible that the children came from particularly caring, or educationally oriented families.

However, when we interviewed the mothers after the observations were completed, we asked them why they sent their child to the school. The majority of the middle-class mothers replied that they had decided to send their child to a nursery school, and had then looked for a suitable school, and consulted their friends, etc. The majority of the working-class mothers said that they had simply noticed the school, which was near their home. The working-class child's enrollment thus seemed to depend more on the school's location than on parental educational policy. These children were probably typical of the majority of working-class children who attend half-day nursery school, and who are nevertheless evaluated by their teachers as needing language enrichment.

We observed in the children's homes for two consecutive afternoons from about 1 p.m. to 3:30 p.m., but used only the second day's data. In the school, we observed for three consecutive mornings from about 9 a.m. to 11:30 a.m. using only the second and third day's data. (It was necessary to collect an extra day's data at school, because the number of adult-child conversations was much smaller.) Because the pilot sessions had shown that large variations in the amount of adult-child talk were caused by the presence of husbands and visitors, we asked the mother to select days for recording when she did not expect any outside guests to be present. Further details of the method and equipment used are reported by Hughes et al. (1979).

Our first concern in analyzing the data was to compare the amount of adult-child talk at home and at school. We first divided the transcript into conversations, defined as episodes of talk on the same subject, ended by a change of subject or by adult or child moving out of earshot. The hourly rate of adult-child conversations in working-class and middle-class homes was almost identical—about 27 conversations per hour—compared with about 10 conversations per hour at school.

Not only were there many more adult-child conversations at home, but the home conversations in both social classes on an average lasted twice as long as those at school. On an average, home conversations lasted for 16 turns, school conversations for 8 turns. (A turn of speech is what is said by one person until another person starts to talk.) Nearly two-thirds of the school conversations, but only two-fifths of the home conversations, lasted for 6 turns or fewer.

These two findings were not unexpected, given the less desirable ratio of adults to children at school, and the obligation of the staff to distribute their attention among the entire class. Typically, the teacher would move from child to child, making a suggestion, giving encouragement, or asking a question. The following conversation is very typical of the briefer school conversations:

(**W.C.** is working-class child; **M.C.** is middle-class child.)

Conversation 1
W.C. Child: (approaching teacher, who is standing around, generally supervising) Had my milk.
Staff: Good girl. Joan's helping Miss Brown move the boxes. Would you like to go and help?
W.C. Child: I drank all my milk up.
Staff: Did you really?
W.C. Child: Mm.
Staff: That was very quick, you didn't take a long time, did you? (child runs outside)

Of course, many conversations at home were equally brief, or briefer:

Conversation 2
Mother: (cutting up frozen meat) Oh, that's cold!
W.C. Child: (eating her lunch, watching mother) What is?
Mother: This is.

Conversation 3
Mother: (referring to the child's two-year-old brother) He must be pretty desperate.
M.C. Child: Pretty desperate! What is pretty desperate?
Mother: It means he needs to go to the loo. Quite quickly.

Often, however, it seemed that the brevity of the teacher's conversation stemmed not only from her need to distribute her attention, but also from a desire to see that the child became engaged in another activity, as in Conversation 1. Some of the longest school conversations occurred on the rare occasions when a teacher was engaged in an activity, e.g., constructing play materials, and the child was watching her. At home, the mother, the child, and the activity remained static for much longer periods. This meant not only that the conversation was able to continue longer, but also that a topic of conversation would often recur. Thus the topic of the frozen meat, Conversation 2, recurred at intervals until the mother had finished her task. Generally, however, the longest conversations occurred not when the child was watching an adult, and certainly not when an adult was watching a child, but when a joint activity was in progress. This was partly because adult and child were brought together by the activity, and partly because the activity required communication. Joint activity occurred about six times as often per hour in homes of both social classes as at school. Reading and discussing a book was the joint activity associated with the longest conversations both at home and at school.

Some conversations we recorded were lengthy due to the nature of the material discussed. Does it matter how long a conversation lasts? This surely depends on the function it serves. A brief conversation may suffice for demands to be made and either met or denied, encouragement to be given, suggestions to be made, information or orders to be given, and even for a question to be answered. But any deep exchange of meaning takes time to achieve, especially if misunderstandings are to be resolved, and control is to be challenged and explained. In Conversation 4, for example, the mother expands her initially cryptic pronouncement in response to persistent questioning by her somewhat anxious child.

Conversation 4
(The lady in question is a speech therapist. The child had recently had her hearing tested.)
Mother: Joan, you've got to go and see another lady on Tuesday.
W.C. Child: What lady?
Mother: Another lady wants to hear you.
W.C. Child: What lady?
Mother: The lady at the clinic wants to hear you speak on Tuesday.
W.C. Child: Is that where Ann goes?
Mother: No, where you got your ears tested. She's going to learn you how to say your words properly. She's going to say them, and you've got to say them after her.
W.C. Child: I don't know all the words.
Mother: Yeah. But she's going to learn you. She's going to teach them to you.
W.C. Child: What's her name?

Mother: Miss Jenkins.
W.C. Child: And that's where I got my ears tested?
Mother: Where you got your ears tested.
W.C. Child: That's where I'm going.
Mother: Mm.

The mother could have given all the information clearly and briefly at the outset, but it seems possible that the active "working over" of the material by the child was an effective way of helping her to understand it.

Similarly, the verbal disputes which were a marked feature of some mother-child relationships, especially in working-class homes, often involved the mother in eventual explanations, and must surely have played an important role in advancing the children's understanding, particularly of family relationships.

Conversation 5
W.C. Child: Mum, can I go down the shop with you?
Mother: Not now.
W.C. Child: Why? Please Mummy?
Mother: Not now. (child starts crying) Haven't had Daddy's money yet.
W.C. Child: I've got no money.
Mother: No. I haven't got enough to get my shopping. Patsy's just taken five pounds. If she's got some she'll bring some change back. It's not enough to get all that (mother points to shopping list). Is it?
W.C. Child: No.
Mother: See? So when Daddy gets paid I'll get some more money and then I'll go.
W.C. Child: Yeah.

Both disputes and persistent questioning by the child rarely occurred at school. Middle-class and working-class children asked questions at about the same rate both at home and at school, but they asked about 26 questions per hour at home contrasted only with about 2 questions per hour at school.

We divided the children's questions into those which arose in relation to adult control (questioning either the control or the justification), questions which arose because of the need of some activity (e.g., "Where are the scissors?"), and curiosity questions. The proportion of questions arising because of the need of some activity was twice as great at school as at home; correspondingly, curiosity questions and questions about control were relatively infrequent at school compared to home. This was particularly true in the case of the working-class children. At home 53 percent of their questions were curiosity questions, and only 34 percent were concerned with the needs of an activity; at school 70 percent were concerned with the needs of an activity, and only 24 percent of their questions were curiosity questions. At both home and school, the average number of questions per conversation was highest in conversations about books, and then in conversations about past and future events.

At school, it was the adult rather than the child who asked the question, and a typical school conversation consisted of a series of questions from the staff, answered rather briefly by the child. Conversation 6 is not atypical.

Conversation 6
Teacher: What color's that you're putting on now? (child is scattering flakes of paint on glue to make a pattern)
W.C. Child: I got . . .
Teacher: What color is that, Mary?
W.C. Child: I don't know—blue.
Teacher: It's a blue color.
W.C. Child: Blue color.
Teacher: Can you lift the paper up?
W.C. Child: No.
Teacher: It is very flimsy? Oh, it's stuck. Why does the paint stick to the paper?
W.C. Child: Glue.
Teacher: Because of the glue. Wouldn't be able to stick to the paper if the glue wasn't there. What color's that you're putting on now?
W.C. Child: Blue.
Teacher: No, that's red.
W.C. Child: Red.
Teacher: That one's blue, that one's yellow, and now you're putting on red (pointing to colors).

Conversation 6 is entirely sustained by the teacher. That is, the child's contribution consists only of answering the questions, or repeating the teacher's remarks—the child does not ask a question or make a demand or a spontaneous comment. In contrast, the home conversations, e.g., Conversations 4 and 5, show a nearly even balance between mother and child. We divided the conversations into those sustained by the child (i.e., those in which more than one-half of the turns contained questions or spontaneous comments by the child) and those sustained by the adult. We found that in homes of both social classes nearly one-half of the conversations were sustained by the children, but at school the proportion was only about one-fifth. The contrast was particularly evident with the working-class children, who sustained 48 percent of the conversations at home, but only 15 percent at school.

The greater equality of the conversational relationship of adult and child at home appeared in another aspect of the conversations—the amount of speech which each contributed. At school, the teachers used nearly three times as many words per turn as the children (on an average, about 14 words per turn compared to 5 per turn by the children), but working-class mothers used only 7 words per turn, and middle-class mothers used 9, their children used 6.

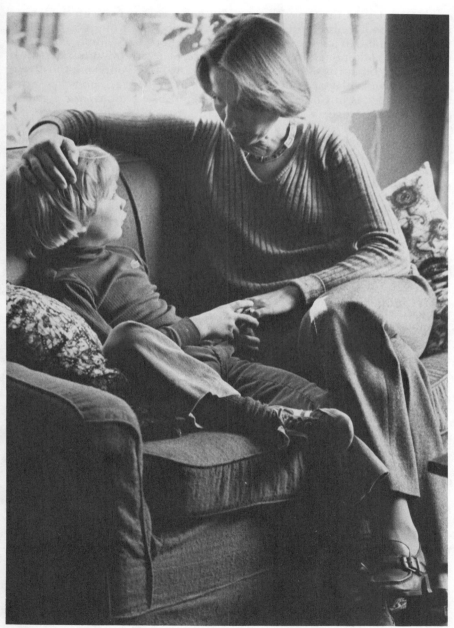

At home, conversations were more frequent, longer, and more evenly balanced between adult and child than those at school. A wider range of topics was discussed, and the children asked many more questions.

The richness of the topics discussed at home contrasted with the limited range at school is also illustrated in Conversations 1 through 6. We found that over one-half of the conversations at school with adults concerned play, and an additional one-fifth were concerned with physical care (washing, putting on aprons, drinking milk, etc.). At home, only one-third were concerned with play activities; other activities and speech about past and future events (as in Conversations 2, 3, 4, and 5) accounted for a greater proportion of conversation at home than at school. Eight percent of the conversations at home, but only 1 percent at school, were concerned with past events, or plans for the future. This difference was not surprising, because conversation at school tends to be centered around the child's ongoing play activity. In British nursery schools, excursions outside the school are unusual, and, apart from Christmas and Easter celebrations, each week at school is very similar. Yet clarifying the relationship between the children's present and past experiences, and projecting future activities, are important ways of helping children make sense of their world.

Conversation 7
(mother and child watching TV film of horses)
Mother: Look!
W.C. Child: Two two two.
Mother: No, it's three, it's five. Look, there's two behind. We saw them, didn't we? In Brockwell Park.
W.C. Child: Yeah. We sit down.
Mother: Yes. And Ruth went to sleep, didn't she?
W.C. Child: Yeah. And I was in the push chair.
Mother: I don't remember that. What did Ruth do then? Daddy carried Ruth, did he? (child nods)

Even when staff at school attempt to carry out this function for children, relating their present and past or future experiences, they are handicapped by ignorance of the small details of the children's lives.

Conversation 8
(child is playing with doll's house)
Staff: Have you got your own bedroom at home?
W.C. Child: Yes.
Staff: How nice. What's in your bedroom?
W.C. Child: Um. . . . .toys.
Staff: Toys, what else? What do you sleep on?
W.C. Child: A bed.
Staff: A bed. Have you got a dressing table?
W.C. Child: No.
Staff: No? No? What do you put all your clothes in?
W.C. Child: Er. . . . a dressing table (hesitantly).
Staff: A dressing table. Has it got a mirror?

W.C. Child: Yes.
Staff: Yes. How beautiful, aren't you lucky?

The most striking finding of our study then was that there were large differences between many aspects of adult-child conversations at home and at school, though social-class differences were relatively small or absent. This is not to say that there were no differences between working-class and middle-class conversations at home. Of the findings reported here, there were social-class differences in the proportion of conversations concerned with the past and future, and in the context in which the children's questions arose. A greater proportion of the middle-class children's questions were curiosity questions, while a larger proportion of the working-class children's questions arose in the context of control.

Social-class differences were also found in the range of information given to the child, and the complexity of the language used by mother and child. These differences were, however, relatively small and few in number, compared with the much larger differences between home and school conversations. At home, conversations were more frequent, longer, and more evenly balanced between adult and child than those at school, a wider range of topics was discussed, and the children asked many more questions.

It is understandable that a teacher with an entire class to look after should hold fewer and briefer conversations with children than their parents. It is also to be expected that because the children's relationship with their teachers are more distant and less trusting than with the parents, the children will contribute less to the conversation at school, and ask fewer questions. Nor, because of the teacher's ignorance of the children's lives outside school, can she or he be expected to duplicate the parents' ability to integrate aspects of the child's experience. A teacher concerned with promoting play activities is unlikely to generate as wide a range of topics for conversation as parents whose daily responsibilities involve cleaning, shopping, cooking, baby care, budgeting, and social relationships with other adults. Once made, these points of difference seem obvious, yet it is not often acknowledged that they imply an educational advantage to parents. Because of children's greater readiness to communicate at home, not only do they get more practice in dialogue with an experienced talker, but a deeper exchange of meaning can take place. This is because children's spontaneous comments and questions serve to focus adult speech on what is of real concern to the child. It is also because children's uncertainties, confusions, and misunderstandings can only be revealed and clarified in the course of a relatively long and free discussion.

The notion that teachers should advise parents on how to talk to their children therefore seems unnecessary. This is not only because of the obvious superiority in many respects of conversation at home, but because how and why parents talk to their children is the result of many complex factors, notably, status relationships within the family, and also what is important to them to communicate. This in turn is likely to depend on a set of underlying attitudes, including their belief about what their children are going to need to function effectively in society. Intervention at a superficial level—e.g., injunctions to use more complex speech forms when talking to children, seem likely, therefore, to be ineffective.

It is true that our study children lived in tolerable housing, in two-parent families with three or fewer children. Very different findings might have been obtained in large, stress-filled families.

What implications does our study have for teachers? First, the data suggested that it is unwise to be critical about the language environment of children's homes, unless one has more evidence than is usually available to the school. The contrary position, that children's homes are likely to be providing them with rich and meaningful language experiences, might be not only more accurate, but may also form the basis for more fruitful cooperation between teachers and parents. Second, it would seem important to be aware of the extent that young children's conversation is influenced by situational constraints. The children in our study who were reluctant to talk to the teacher, answered her briefly, and rarely if ever asked her questions, bombarded their mothers with conversation and questions at home.

Can teachers learn from parents about talking to children? The restrictions on teachers have already been discussed: the poor adult-child ratio, the teacher's relative ignorance of the child's out-of-school life, the social distance between staff and child, and the narrow focus of interests at school.

Some of these restrictions are self-imposed—e.g., nursery activity does not have to focus so closely on play; teachers could become better acquainted with children in their homes. There appeared to be an additional restriction, which was the staff's conception of what the children should be doing. Many school conversations seemed to be rapidly terminated, not by other demands being made on the teacher, but by her suggestion to the child to start or continue a play activity. That is, the underlying strategy of the teacher seemed to be to involve the child in play, alone or with other children, rather than in discussion with an adult. The long conversations at school with any substantial contribution from the child occurred primarily when a story was being read to one or two children, when teacher and child were engaged in some joint activity, such as playing, or when the teacher was engaged in some activity, e.g., sewing or constructing play materials which kept her in one place for a prolonged period of time.

The choice of strategy depends on one's educational priorities. Present nursery-school practice is well designed to give children play experiences with other children, and with a wide variety of equipment; it is less suited to encouraging adult-child conversation and activities other than play. For those families who sent their children to nursery school to enable them to play with other children, and who provided plenty of adult-child talk and nonplay activities at home, present nursery school practice might be considered well suited to their needs. An educational strategy for children from large families, or for those attending a day care center for eight or more hours a day might, however, be rather different. In either case, a valid understanding of what both home and school are providing seems a prerequisite to devising educational goals and strategies.

References

Bullock Report: A Language for Life. London: Her Majesty's Stationary Office, 1975.

Hughes, M.; Tizard, B.; Carmichael, H.; and Pinkerton, G. "Recording Children's Conversations at Home and at Nursery School: A Technique and Some Methodological Considerations. *Journal of Child Psychology and Psychiatry* 20, no. 3 (1979):225-232.

Tizard, B.; Philps, J.; and Plewis, I. "Staff Behaviour in Pre-School Centres." *Journal of Child Psychology and Psychiatry* 17 (1975): 21-33.

Tizard, B. "Carry on Communicating." *Times Educational Supplement,* no. 19 (1978).

Tizard, B.; Carmichael, H.; Hughes, M.; and Pinkerton, G. "Four-Year-Olds Talking to Mothers and Teachers." In *Language and Language Disorders in Childhood,* ed. L. A. Hersov. Oxford: Pergamon Press, 1980.

Wells, G. "Language Development in Pre-School Children." Unpublished paper, University of Bristol, 1975.

Wootton, A. "Talk in the Homes of Young Children." *Sociology* 8, no. 2 (1974): 277-295.

Part II
Developing a Program

Courtney B. Cazden

3.
Suggestions for Curriculum and Teaching

This section contains a diverse group of chapters that contain rich suggestions for curriculum and teaching in oral language education during the preschool years. No one point of view is held by all the authors. Yet all the ideas relate to the more general discussion in Part I.

In Chapter 4, Bartlett provides a critical analysis of commercially available language curricula: their goals, interaction patterns, and provisions for instructional management. Three programs for parents are included. While her list of specific programs is apt to become out-of-date, her discussion should continue to be helpful in evaluating and selecting future programs.

In the first chapter, I stressed the importance of communication skills. In Chapter 5, Gleason describes how she taught more explicit referential communication to preschool children. In Chapter 6, Mattick asks what would happen if teachers provided real communication instead of "language treatment," and she suggests specific do's and don'ts to facilitate that communication.

One objective of some programs is to improve children's competence in understanding and speaking standard English. Because I am not aware of any evidence that speaking a nonstandard dialect is in and of itself any cognitive liability, questions about dialect have to be considered as value questions. Such value questions should be decided by the people most closely concerned—parents and representatives from the children's community. Chapter 7, "Making It and Going Home," reports one attempt to find out what kind of language education people in a Boston community would like. Since that was done, two similar studies have been conducted in other parts of the country: by Granger (1976) in Georgia, and Hoover (1978) in the Bay area of northern California. Chapter 8, "Language Development in Day Care Programs," also focuses on the language of Black children, but many of the ideas have more general application.

This entire book is limited to questions about the English language in early childhood education, and it does not pretend to address adequately the needs of children from non-English-speaking communities. But Chapter 9 by Gonzalez-Mena is an excellent beginning for planning how best to combine English and the child's native language in a preschool program.

We also do not discuss the special needs of children whose language is delayed or impaired. Fortunately, there is now a comprehensive Head Start handbook, *Mainstreaming Preschoolers: Children with Speech and Language Impairments* (Liebergott and Favors 1978). Another book, *Special Education and Development: Perspectives on Young Children with Special Needs* (Meisels 1979), does not focus on language needs per se, but provides a comprehensive discussion of the benefits of including children with special needs in open education settings. For teachers and parents of deaf children, two books are especially recommended: *Deaf Like Me* (Spradley and Spradley 1978) and *The Logic of Action: Young Children at Work* (Hawkins 1974). The language curriculum for hearing-impaired children by Blackwell, Engen, Fischgrund, and Zarcadoolas (1978) includes a chapter on preschool and kindergarten. I am sorry that the inclusion of sign language in a total communication program is not as evident in the book as it is in The Rhode Island School for the Deaf, an exciting school where the curriculum was developed.

References

Blackwell, P. M.; Engen, E.; Fischgrund, J. E.; and Zarcadoolas, C. *Sentences and Other Systems: A Language and Learning Curriculum for Hearing-Impaired Children.* Washington, D.C.: The Alexander Graham Bell Association for the Deaf, 1978.

Granger, R. C. "The Nonstandard Speaking Child: Myths Past and Present." *Young Children* 31, no. 6 (September 1976): 479-485.

*Hawkins, F. P. *The Logic of Action: Young Children at Work.* Revised ed. New York: Pantheon, 1974.

Hoover, M. R. "Community Attitudes Toward Black English." *Language in Society* 7 (1978): 65-87.

Liebergott, J., and Favors, A., Jr. *Mainstreaming Preschoolers: Children with Speech and Language Impairments.* Washington, D.C.: U.S. Department of Health, Education and Welfare, 1978.

Meisels, S. J., ed. *Special Education and Development: Perspectives on Young Children with Special Needs.* Baltimore: University Park Press, 1979.

*Spradley, T. S., and Spradley, J. P. *Deaf Like Me.* New York: Random House, 1978.

Elsa Jaffe Bartlett

4.
Selecting an Early Childhood Language Curriculum

The first edition of this chapter was published in 1972 when commercially published preschool language programs were just beginning to appear. At that time, about 25 to 30 programs were available—none with a copyright date that was more than three years old. Although all programs purported to foster children's language development, no two of them went on to define language in quite the same way. Some emphasized syntax or vocabulary development; others stressed interactional patterns. In some cases, language was thought to develop through rote repetition; in others, through discussion or role play. Apart from this, programs differed in terms of cost, amount of time required, type of teacher's guide, and type of children's materials. Since then, publication of classroom programs has burgeoned and there are now also books of language activities for parents. Several excellent publications provide detailed schemes for evaluating the language of young learners and a few attempt to help teachers diagnose their own classroom interactions. When we were compiling materials for the first edition, virtually all originated with American educators and most were based on programs designed to improve the language of children who were then called disadvantaged. Today, we have available more programs originating in the English open classrooms, and while the majority of programs still focus on the special needs of inner-city children, some now attempt to reach a much broader range of children.

The variety of programs is no less bewildering than it was in 1972 and the purpose of this paper is still, as it was then, to help the teacher evaluate these various approaches to language curriculum and relate them to what is currently known about language development.

Special thanks are due to Kathy McGeorge and Laurie Scott who selected the programs, analyzed the materials, and provided many valuable suggestions at all stages of the work.

In order to include a wider range of programs, in this edition, we adopted a more flexible set of selection criteria. As in the past, we included only programs designed for use with children between the ages of three and six years. In addition to classroom programs, however, we have included a few programs for parents. These are described at the end of the chapter (pp. 74-75).

Once again, we included only programs which are readily available to the general public, either through commercial publishers or the originating research organization. We included only programs which defined themselves as focusing on language and the development of verbal skills. Programs which seemed aimed primarily at the development of traditional reading readiness skills were not included.

As in the past, we also required that programs provide a systematic curriculum. Because we believed that a curriculum should consist of at least some kind of instructional plan, we took as our minimum criterion for inclusion the requirement that a program provide a teacher's guide with specific procedures designed to guide interactions in the classroom. We had the further requirement that procedures must have been minimally sequenced either in terms of time (e.g., first, second) or difficulty (easy, hard); a two-step series of procedures was taken as minimally acceptable. To qualify under these criteria, a program need not include classroom materials for the children.

The resulting set consists of 27 classroom programs and 3 programs designed for parents. These are listed in Figure 4.1 and described more fully at the end of this chapter (pp. 65-75).

The child as language learner

If research reveals anything about language development, it is that normal, unimpaired children will learn their mother tongue, regardless of experience in school. Children are prodigious language-learners. By the age of 6, for example, it has been estimated that the average child has acquired a vocabulary of 7,800 different words. If we suppose that word-learning begins in earnest at about the age of 12 months, then simple arithmetic leads us to conclude that children are learning new words at the rate of four per day or roughly one for every three waking hours. Although the rates differ somewhat for middle- and lower-class children, there is no question that the lower class (at 3.78 words per day) is every bit as skilled in its learning as middle-class children. Nor is syntactic development any less rapid. By the age of 6 or 7, the young learner will have mastered much of the basic syntax of English.

Language in social and intellectual development

Clearly the learning of language has important ramifications for both social and intellectual development. By enabling us to make our ideas and concepts explicit, language serves to make our intellectual life available to others and provides a means by which others, through discussion and argument, can lead us to amend and extend our notions. At the same time, by attempting to interpret the language of others, we sharpen our own concepts and develop new ones.

Figure 4.1
List of Programs

Classroom programs

ALG. Young. *Amazing Life Games*. Boston: Houghton Mifflin, 1971. $525.00.

BECP. Nedler. *Bilingual Early Childhood Program*. Tex.: Southwest Educational Development, 1973. $620.00.

Blank. Blank. *Teaching Learning in the Preschool: A Dialogue Approach*. Columbus, Ohio: Merrill, 1973. $6.95.

Bowmar. Jaynes; Woodbridge; Curry; and Crume. *Bowmar Early Childhood Series*. Los Angeles: Bowmar, 1968. $390.00.

Concepts. Morris; Hoban; Mully; Davis; Simon; and Carson. *Beginning Concepts: 1 and 2*. Englewood Cliffs, N.J.: Scholastic, 1973. $135.00.

DISTAR. Engelmann and Osborn. *DISTAR, Language 1*. Chicago: Science Research, 1969. $273.00.

Focus. Tough. *Focus on Meaning*. London: George, Allen and Unwin, 1973. $6.50. (Published in the United States as *Talking, Thinking, Growing*. New York: Schocken Books, 1973.)

Goal. Karnes. *Goal Program: Language Development*. East Long Meadow, Mass.: Milton Bradley, 1972. $130.00.

Intellectual Skills. Hobson and McCauley. *Intellectual Skills and Language*. Tucson, Ariz.: Arizona Center for Educational Research and Development, 1976. $3.00.

Kamii and DeVries. Kamii and DeVries. *Physical Knowledge in Preschool Education*. Englewood Cliffs, N.J.: Prentice-Hall, 1978. $12.95.

Kindle. *Kindle Sound-Filmstrip Series. Units 2 and 5*. Englewood Cliffs, N.J.: Scholastic, 1974. $119.00.

Lavatelli. Lavatelli. *Early Childhood Curriculum*. Boston: American Science and Engineering, 1973. $323.45.

Minicourse. Ward and Kelley. *Developing Children's Oral Language, Minicourse 2*. Beverly Hills, Calif.: Macmillan Educational Services, 1971. $6.00 plus $206.75 film rental fees.

Murphy and O'Donnell. Murphy and O'Donnell. *Developing Oral Language with Young Children*. Cambridge, Mass.: Educator's Publishing Service, 1971. $11.50.

Prices are for materials for groups of 20 or more students. The name in bold type is the one used when referring to the program in this chapter.

Oral English. Thomas and Allen. *Oral English.* Oklahoma City, Okla.: Economy, 1972. $213.84.

Peabody. Dunn; Horton; and Smith. *Peabody Language Development Kit, Level P.* Circle Pines, Minn.: American Guidance Service, 1968. $192.00.

SELF. Monolakes and Scian. *Self.* Morristown, N.J.: Silver Burdett, 1974. $198.00.

Simonds. Simonds. *Language Skills for the Young Child.* San Francisco: R & E Research Associates, 1975. $4.00.

SWRL. Southwest Regional Laboratories. *Communication Skills Program: Expressive Language, Blocks 1 and 2.* Lexington, Mass.: Ginn, 1975. $43.70.

Talk Reform. Gahagan and Gahagan. *Talk Reform.* Beverly Hills, Calif.: Sage, 1970. $5.95.

Talkabout. Pasamanick. *Talkabout.* Little Neck, N.Y.: Center for Media Development, 1976. $19.95.

Talking and Learning. Tough. *Talking and Learning.* London: Ward Lock Educational, 1977. Approximately $6.00.

Target. Novakovich; Smith; and Teegarden. *Target on Language Grammar Program.* Bethesda, Md.: Christ Church Child Center, 1977. $5.00.

*Weikart. Weikart; Rogers; Adcock; and McClelland. *The Cognitively Oriented Curriculum.* Washington, D.C.: National Association for the Education of Young Children, 1971. $5.40.

Whispers. Markavitch. *Whispers: Language Skills.* Pleasantville, N.Y.: Readers Digest Services, 1977. $32.00.

Wordworld. Lane; Sucher; and McCay. *Wordworld.* Oklahoma City, Okla.: Economy, 1976. $210.00.

Yonemura. Yonemura. *Developing Language Programs for Young Disadvantaged Children.* New York: Teacher's College Press, 1969. $11.50.

Parent programs

Braun, D. *200 Ways to Help Children Learn While You're at It.* Reston, Va.: Reston Publishing, 1976. $9.95.

Karnes, M. *Learning Language at Home.* Reston, Va.: Council for Exceptional Children, 1977. $35.00.

Pushaw, D. *Teach Your Child to Talk.* Fairfield, N.J.: Cebco Standard Publishing, 1977. $175.00 plus $120.00 for film.

A first encounter with a new word can provide the occasion for initial development of a new concept. Each additional encounter can serve to extend and enrich that concept. In this sense, we can see that using and interpreting language can help us bring a kind of order to our experiences. But at the same time as language structures experience, it is easy to see that our social experience structures our language.

---

*Since this review of language curricula was completed, a revised edition of Weikart's curriculum has been published (see references on page 65 under Hohmann, Banet, and Weikart 1979).

Language serves a variety of functions. Through it, we request action or information, make promises, agree, disagree, deny, assert, describe, narrate, and seek support. Most of us participate in a full range of these functions, but we perform them in different contexts. Where we feel powerful, we may make demands or requests. Where confident, we may disagree or argue. Where unsure, we may seek support. In part, our language use is determined by our idiosyncratic and momentary experiences, but it is also determined by our expectations concerning behavior appropriate to our various social roles. In some families, for example, children are insolent if they ask too many questions of adults, while in other families these children are valued as intellectually venturesome. Similarly, in some job roles, workers are considered disloyal if they argue with their boss, while in others they are praised for their creative independence.

Different roles promote different constellations of language functions and these may, in turn, affect the kinds of meanings which are learned and used. We can see this clearly enough if we imagine two young children, each learning the word "why." For both, the word may initially have a global meaning, akin perhaps to the notion tell-me-something. In one case, the child is encouraged to use the word in exploring the environment and after many exchanges begins to realize that "why" can be used to elicit information about both motivation and physical causality. More important, the child will also begin to realize that motivation and physical causality are things that one can obtain information about; they become possible objects of inquiry. Thus, the child has learned both a set of meanings for a word and a set of goals that can be achieved through the act of requesting information. In the case of the second child there is no such encouragement: Other members of the child's speech community see a child's use of "why" as something of a nuisance. The word will eventually elicit a sufficient number of responses for the child to learn aspects of its meaning although it may take longer for the child to accomplish this learning. But more important, the child may learn that motivation and physical causality are not appropriate objects of inquiry. It is not that such a child would never learn to request information, but such a child may fail to learn that these are valued objects of such an inquiry. In this sense, then, we can say that to learn one's mother tongue is not simply to learn a vocabulary and syntax, but also to learn a set of potentials for meaning.

This is no less true at school than at home: As children learn the behavior associated with being good students, they are learning an appropriate set of uses for language which affect both the vocabulary and syntax assimilated by children. For the monolingual child, we tend to underplay the differences between home and school languages but in fact, for any child the two are likely to differ in fairly important ways. Despite the obvious similarities of vocabulary and grammar, the school presents the child with both a new social order and a new set of contexts for language use. Children who have learned a language which enables them to interact with family and friends must now learn to interact with those cast in the different social roles of teacher and classmate; regardless of cultural similarities or differences between the child and the individuals who happen to be cast in these roles, the roles themselves represent important new constellations of language features.

In evaluating or developing language programs, then, it will be at least as important to consider how the role of learner is construed and the range of functions to which children's language is put, as it is to consider explicit vocabulary and syntax. Depending on their lesson topics, language programs may emphasize the physical properties of objects or the nature of social interactions as interesting objects of inquiry. At the same time, depending on the dominant teacher-student interactions, programs may convey very different notions about the role of the student. For example, programs that emphasize word- or sentence-repetitions may convey the notion that the student is to duplicate previously known and highly specified information, while programs emphasizing a more spontaneous flow of discussion may convey the notion that the student's job is to come up with a new or previously unarticulated aspect of the topic. The point is not that one set of topics or type of teacher-child interaction is necessarily better than another, but that different programs convey different notions about language and the context of language use and that these differences are likely to add up to rather different embodiments of the role of the student.

For this reason, it will be important in our curriculum analyses to characterize not only a program's vocabulary and syntax, but also the topic or focus of a lesson and the dominant type of teacher-child interaction. We will begin with a discussion of topic, followed by a consideration of the role of vocabulary and syntax, and an analysis of the dominant patterns of teacher-child interaction in these programs. Following this, we will discuss aspects of instructional management: the extent to which material is presequenced, the type of evaluation provided, and the type of information provided in the teachers' guides. We will conclude with some general comments about program evaluation.

Curriculum analyses
Topic
A few programs in our sample fail to structure their lessons around particular topics of inquiry. Instead, their curricula seem to be organized around language patterns themselves, with sequences of lessons organized around practice with various syntactic structures such as passives, negatives, or comparatives. (Six of the 27 programs were of this type; they are listed in Figure 4.2, p. 39.) For the most part, however, programs in our sample seem to be structured around one of two topics of inquiry—either they emphasize certain mathematical/logical relations or they focus on various aspects of social behavior (see Figure 4.3).

Mathematical/logical relations. Many programs focus on the use of language to define sets and classes, to describe comparisons of size or quantity,

---

Figure 4.2

Programs which Emphasize Syntax

DISTAR

Murphy and O'Donnell

Oral English

Target

Wordworld

Yonemura

---

and to express logical necessities. Additionally, children learn to interpret language intended to isolate or focus attention on aspects of a problem's solution, to verbalize certain problem-solving rules and procedures, and to communicate the outcome of their inquiry into these relations. In the process, children are thought to be acquiring the notion that these relations and the deductive reasoning by which they are achieved can be possible objects of inquiry and thus part of the child's developing potential for comprehending meaning. Among other things, this is intended to give children adequate preparation for the elementary science and mathematics curricula.

Social/psychological relations. As we can see from Figure 4.3 (p. 40), 4 programs give primary emphasis to social/psychological relations, with 2 focusing on interactional processes, and 2 on reasoning about social interactions; while of the 17 programs emphasizing mathematical/logical reasoning, 6 also give additional emphasis to social relations.

In programs which emphasize social reasoning, children are asked to interpret the feelings, point of view, and motivations of others (including storybook characters); to predict outcomes and generate hypotheses about events; to summarize events; to identify whole-part and functional relations; and identify absurdities based on these relations. In most cases, children are asked to discuss material presented in pictures and storybooks. While they are required to name items in the pictures and story illustrations correctly, there is relatively little emphasis on learning precise syntax and vocabulary; as long as children can communicate their ideas, their language is deemed functionally adequate. Although they are required to communicate the results of their reasoning, they are not often required to verbalize problem-solving rules and procedures.

Following the theory that it is somehow easier for children to reason

Figure 4.3

Distribution of Program Topics

Program names	Topic type		
	Math/logic	Social/psychological	
		Social reasoning	Social interactions
ALG	P*		
BECP	P		
Blank	P		
Intellectual Skills	P		
Lavatelli	P		
Minicourse	P		
Peabody	P		
Talkabout	P		
Talking and Learning	P		
Weikart	P		
Whispers	P		
Concepts	P	S*	
Focus	P	S	
GOAL	P		S
Kamii and DeVries	P	S	
Kindle	P	S	
Simonds	P		S
Bowmar	S	P	
SELF	S	P	
SWRL		S	P
Talk Reform	S		P

*P = primary emphasis (most frequent type of topic in program)
 S = secondary emphasis (second-most frequent topic in program)

about characters in the here-and-now, such programs often follow a strategy of setting first lessons in the context of a preschool classroom and gradually shifting the setting to the larger community. Generally, the resulting materials are similar in content and focus to those which the child will later encounter in a basic reading program. It may be partly with this in mind that the materials have been selected.

In other programs, it is the process of social interaction itself which is emphasized. Inquiry centers around a communication enacted by the children either in the form of role play, dramatization, nonnarrative exposition, or description. Often, children are asked to solve socially based problems through the use of some sort of improvisation. These problems are similar to those described in the preceding section, depending heavily on children's understanding of motivation, appropriate social behavior, and the roles undertaken by others in various social interactions, both at school and in the larger community. However, here the emphasis is on process rather than analysis and so, while children are asked to interpret the reactions of others, to predict outcomes, and to generate hypotheses about events, this type of thinking occurs as children actively pursue various communicative purposes in their dramatizations. The purposes themselves usually include asking for help, getting attention, persuading, winning an argument, providing an adequate explanation, negotiating a quarrel, and initiating an inquiry. These aspects of language behavior may occasionally be overlooked, but some children may indeed have difficulty in school precisely because they do not know how to accomplish these purposes through language. The goal of these programs is to help children adopt better communication strategies. This is less important in a traditional teacher-dominated setting, but can be crucial in an open classroom where children have much more responsibility for making their needs known and finding out what they need to know.

In addition to developing communication strategies, these programs also provide children with practice in making certain kinds of abstractions: When a child enacts a role, she or he must be able to abstract the central or salient characteristics of the person whose role will be played and organize these characteristics so as to reproduce or represent the character through appropriate behavior.

One potential problem with programs that emphasize social relations is that they sometimes portray values, situations, and customs that are unfamiliar or even alienating to many children. For example, in the Bowmar program, the children are well dressed and living in what appears to be a middle-income suburb in California. There are only two or three pictures of low-income dwellings, no stories about families with large numbers of children, and none where a woman is head of the household. In GOAL, the families are virtually all White. Pictures of community helpers included only two women (the nurse and the teacher). Needless to say, the doctor is a White male. In Peabody, it is the female who stays home while the males go out to work; no other family arrangements are mentioned. Again, while the nurse and teacher are female, the doctor, dentist, police officer, and farmer are all male. In Talk Reform, the sex stereotyping takes a more subtle tone. For example, "Almost any day, children, *particularly boys,* will bring some object, piece of equipment, toy or novelty . . . (p. 27, italics ours)." Needless to say, this stereotyping will be offensive to many people.

One result of such stereotyping is that many children may have difficulty relating to these materials and using their own experiences to solve the problems presented in these programs. They may be confused by the discussion questions suggested in the teachers' guides or lose interest altogether. But even more important is the fact that such stereotyping provides misinformation for all children concerning many important aspects of their culture.

Most programs, though, present a reasonably multicultural (and in a few cases nonsexist) environment and a few seem to make a special effort to promote an awareness and genuine appreciation of cultural diversity. Oral English and BECP take considerable pains to discuss the special languages and cultures of various groups. Blank and Intellectual Skills are also sensitive to language diversity. Wordworld presents a nice variety of life-styles and occupational roles (the school principal is a Black female; the telephone operator is a White male). The SELF program indicates that sex role de-stereotyping is one of its explicit goals.

It is clear from Figure 4.3 (p. 40) that social and mathematical relations are not equally represented among the topics of these programs. In the majority of cases, a program which places primary emphasis on mathematical/logical relations does not emphasize social/psychological reasoning. The reverse, however, almost never occurs: If a program gives primary emphasis to social/psychological relations, it almost always has a secondary emphasis on mathematical/logical reasoning. This suggests that mathematical/logical reasoning is considered necessary even in programs which emphasize inquiry into social interactions. It is not clear why this should be the case, but the assumption seems to be that children in the preschool years require special practice constructing and encoding these kinds of relations. Certainly there is much in the literature on cognitive development (and especially the Piagetian literature) to support such a position. What is less clear, however, is whether special practice is also needed in the construction and encoding of the relations encountered in programs that emphasize social reasoning.

Vocabulary

The vocabulary in these programs depends to a large extent on the dominant topic or subject matter. Programs which emphasize social/psychological relations tend to include words which describe everyday objects and events (e.g., clothing, kitchen utensils, furniture, writing or drawing implements, and traffic signals); motives and feelings; social interactions; and occasionally, occupational roles.

Programs which emphasize mathematical/logical relations generally include words that describe quantitative, spatial, or temporal relations. Variously dubbed "basic cognitive concepts" or "the cognitive code," these include prepositions and adverbs which refer to spatial relationships; names of common geometric shapes; prepositions, adverbs, and conjunctions referring to temporal relationships; as well as words which refer to certain sensory experiences such as textures and colors. It is not altogether clear why these words are so consistently singled out for special attention, but two reasons seem plausible. First, each group is a relatively limited set of words (e.g., there are only 12 or so common color names, 32 prepositions). Second, most of these words are easy to illustrate with pictures or three-dimensional materials (and those which are not—such as the temporal words *early* and *late*—are included less frequently)'. Educators claim that these are words somehow basic to further school learning. There is no question that they provide a language useful for describing certain kinds of visual displays, particularly those found in mathematics and science programs.

The words themselves stand for relationships of varying complexity. Certainly, children do not learn the full adult meaning of all terms in the preschool years nor the implications of those terms in all logical or syntactic contexts. They may, for example, have grasped the notion that *some* and *all* refer to quantity, but have difficulty interpreting a sentence such as *All daisies are flowers, but not all flowers are daisies.* Or again, the words *before* and *after* may be interpreted as referring to the order in which events are mentioned rather than the order in which they occur and, as a result, children may interpret the command *"Before you open the window shut the door,"* to mean that the window is to be opened first. There are, of course, many examples of how children incompletely understand relational terms in the work of Piaget and his colleagues. Additional examples are emerging from studies of children's semantic development. Initially, for example, the word *tall* may simply mean *big* and only later take on its full meaning. Similarly, children may at first use color words indiscriminately to refer to any hue and only gradually acquire the notion that each refers to a specific one.

We have already noted that children acquire vocabulary at a prodigious rate, but as these examples suggest, complete mastery is not likely to occur overnight. But if full learning takes time, it is also clear that some initial although fragmentary learning can occur quite rapidly. Indeed, studies in our laboratory have demonstrated that children can attach some appropriate meaning to a word after having heard it just once or twice.

Although we know very little about this initial rapid learning, it appears as if children usually learn something about a word's semantic category (is it a color? a plant? a bird?) and along with that, some information as to its syntactic subcategorization. (For example, that it is similar to other verbs or animate nouns. Children do not learn, of course, to attach labels such as verb or noun to words, but they do seem to use language in terms of such categorizations.) Indeed, it is possible that such fragmentary learning is sufficient to keep a word in the vocabulary for a long period of time. Many of us have entries for words that include little more than the fact that a phonological sequence or string of sounds is a word. I think, for example, of *puce*. I know that *puce* is a color, but I cannot tell you what color it is.

Word learning, then, appears to be a two-phase process. Although some initial learning seems to occur after only a few exposures, it can take months or even years before the child has understood the subtle relations that can exist between one word and others within the same domain (tall, long, wide, thick). What is eventually understood, of course, depends on what the child encounters and it is here that the school can be particularly helpful—by providing opportunities for the child to encounter these words in many new and varied contexts. We should keep this in mind when we examine the goals of language programs. Many seem to provide only a limited exposure to a few simple contexts. Children may, for example, be required to do no more than identify a few similar illustrations as indications of a concept—enough to establish an initial acquaintance with a word (should that be necessary) but hardly enough to help the child develop an extended meaning. (This is true, for example, of the material provided by Wordworld, which uses only a few similar workbook pictures to illustrate the meaning of words.) Others provide a richer experience through tasks designed to give children practice with the underlying concepts and logical relations in a variety of contexts. (See Blank's suggestions for developing word meanings.)

It is not at all clear. A Piagetian would point out that the development of word meanings is limited by the concepts available to a child, for in the end, a word can mean only what a child can conceptualize. A Vygotskian, on the other hand, would say that while this may be true, an encounter with a new word or an old word in a new context can be the occasion for the child to begin to develop a new concept or extend an immature one. A balance between new input and available interpretive apparatus is clearly important for language learning, but unfortunately, research has little to tell us about how an optimal balance can be achieved. At present, conscientious teachers must rely (as they always have) on intuition and their previous teaching experience.

Syntax

To the extent that children speak, they will be using syntax, although the actual patterns will depend to a large extent on the content they are encoding (e.g., comparisons, predictions, sensory descriptions). In many programs the child's focus is not on the patterns themselves, but on the content of the communication, and while a child may occasionally be required to recast an utterance in a different form or repeat a particular phrasing, this is incidental to other aspects of the child's interaction. In six programs, however, the syntax itself becomes the focus of attention (see Figure 4.2). In two (Wordworld and DISTAR) there is some secondary emphasis on social or mathematical relations but for four (Yonemura, Target, Oral English, and Murphy and O'Donnell) the focus is almost entirely on the syntax itself. Two of these, Oral English and Target, teach a variety of basic syntactic patterns. The rest focus on a limited subset. These include two types, one involving purely grammatical relations (the correct use of auxilliaries and verb inflections to express mood and tense; noun-verb number agreement; and pronominal reference) and the other, sentence forms that seem to be selected for cognitive as well as linguistic purposes (almost as if the syntactic relations are thought to represent reasoning processes as well). Thus, for example, in many of these latter programs where children are asked to repeat conditional sentence structures or use *not* in identity statements, they apparently are thought to be practicing deductive logic or constructing class inclusion relations. DISTAR and Yonemura seem to approach syntax in this way, as do Peabody and Talk Reform.

Several things should be noted about these programs. First, many have been designed specifically for either "disadvantaged" or learning-disabled children. Their purpose has been to provide training in standard English or, as it is sometimes called, "school dialect." The form of the training is usually pattern repetition (see p. 46, 48), a technique often used in second-language programs for older children and adults. It is unclear the extent to which such training is necessary or even advisable with young language learners, especially children who, at three and four years, are still very much in the throes of acquiring their mother tongue. What we know about syntactic development is still too limited for us to make a judgment, but it does seem that parents provide little direct syntactic training during first language acquisition. If they correct a child's speech at all, the corrections seem to be aimed at the truthfulness or social appropriateness of an utterance and not its syntax. It is not at all clear that programs which explicitly direct the child's attention to syntax are any more effective than those which direct attention towards a communication act and only incidentally provide a syntactic model for the child to use in framing the resulting utterance.

The teacher's attention, however, is a different matter for it is quite possible that directing teachers' attention to their own and their pupils' syntax may increase both teachers' awareness of children's current progress and difficulties along with the effectiveness with which their communications foster syntactic development. A number of programs go to considerable length to help teachers achieve an increased awareness of their language as well as that of children. Among these are Focus on Meaning, Blank, Intellectual Skills, and especially Minicourse, which was explicitly designed to help teachers become more aware of their own language while carrying out a language program.

Dominant teacher-pupil interaction

Along with topic, vocabulary, and emphasis on syntax, programs differ in the type of response required from children. These can range from the repetition of words and sentence patterns to improvisations and storytelling. Some programs require children to answer long sequences of teacher-posed questions; in others, children engage in free-ranging spontaneous conversations. In our analyses, we found that certain groups of responses seemed to occur together. Thus, for example, if a program requires much repetition, then children are often also required to answer long sequences of questions posed by the teacher. At the same time, these programs rarely require children to engage in improvisations or role play, make up stories, ask questions, or participate in spontaneous conversations. In looking at activities which clustered together, it is clear that the groupings depend on the extent to which children's activities are initiated and structured by the teacher: at one end of the spectrum, we find highly structured pattern repetitions and at the other, open-ended role plays and story making. Between these extremes are some programs which focus on teacher-directed question-answer sequences and some which emphasize a more spontaneous type of teacher-child discussion.

Pattern repetition
These interactions will typically conform to one of these prototypes:

1. Teacher models a word, sentence pattern, or problem-solving rule; child repeats. (**T:** This ball is round. Now you say it. **C:** This ball is round.)
2. Teacher asks a question; child answers with a previously practiced response. (**T:** What kind of ball is this? **C:** This ball is round.)
3. Child asks a previously practiced question; another child answers with a practiced response. (**C:** What can you say about this? **C:** This ball is round.)

The child's task in this type of interaction is to imitate a model as closely as possible. In certain cases the child may have an opportunity to choose which of several models will be used, but once the child settles on one, the child must follow it precisely. Success, which is judged by the teacher, depends on whether an appropriate model has been chosen and on how accurately it has been imitated.

The teacher's role demands that the teacher initiate and direct the learning. The teacher presents materials, models the language patterns, asks questions, and provides feedback.

Nine programs emphasize pattern repetitions (see Figure 4.4). Most require children to engage in other speaking and listening activities that are highly structured by the teacher: answering teacher-posed sequences of questions, completing sentences, following directions, and identifying elements named or described by the teacher. (Peabody also provides considerable practice with less structured spontaneous discussions.)

As we have already noted, this type of interaction differs considerably from what the language-learning child participates in at home. Parents rarely seem to ask children to repeat or practice sentence structure; even vocabulary seems to receive relatively little explicit attention. Similarly, children have many opportunities to initiate and direct the course of a communication sequence while the adult acts as responder.

Pattern repetition is valuable if language learning is thought to follow a paired-associate paradigm; that is, if the child's task is seen as learning to associate a label with an object or relationship and if this association is

Figure 4.4
Distribution of Interaction Types

Program names*	Interaction types			
	Pattern repetition	*Structured question sequences*	*Single questions/ spontaneous discussion*	*Improvisations and storytelling*
Wordworld	X			
Target	X			
Oral English	X			
Yonemura	X			
GOAL	X	X		
DISTAR	X	X		
Minicourse	X	X		
Talking and Learning	X	X		
Peabody	X		X	
Focus on Meaning		X		
Blank		X		
Talkabout		X		
Lavatelli		X		
Kamii and DeVries		X		
Whispers			X	
Bowmar			X	
Concepts			X	
Kindle			X	
ALG		X		X
Weikart		X		X
BECP			X	X
Simonds			X	X
Intellectual Skills			X	X
Talk Reform			X	X
SELF			X	X
SWRL			X	X

* The Murphy and O'Donnell program is divided into several subsections, each with its own dominant type of teacher-child interaction. The resulting heterogeneity made it impossible to classify the program, as a whole, within this scheme.

thought to be strengthened by many overt repetitions. But there is little evidence to suggest that this provides anything like an adequate explanation of either vocabulary or syntax development. Indeed, recent studies of word learning suggest that children do acquire some word knowledge on the basis of only a few incidental exposures, often without any overt repetition at all on the part of the child.

However, apart from this, repetitive interactions may be valuable for a completely different reason: Because these interactions require that the child respond to some minimum number of teacher questions, we know that each child participating in such a program will have at least some experience with teacher-child question-response interactions. This provides each child with teacher-child verbal contact, insuring that the least communicative children are not overlooked.

One problem with this type of interaction—if used extensively—may involve transfer. Children are using language in a very limited set of communication contexts and, unfortunately, there is not much evidence that they will be able to generalize their language use to other types of contexts. In other words, children may be able to perform well in similar contexts, but may fail to apply what they have learned to situations where role requirements are different—e.g., where they are responsible for initiating and managing their own inquiry.

Structured question sequence

Somewhat less structured than the pattern repetitions are the structured question sequences, intended to model for the child certain problem-solving and reasoning procedures.

The child's task is not to imitate an exact model but to follow certain procedures for organizing and communicating information. The questioning is designed to lead the child through the requisite steps. Extensive repetition is certainly not necessary on any given occasion, although the teacher may take a few minutes to rehearse a new word or even a sentence with a child. Indeed, there is often no right answer to a problem and any answer which the child can justify within the problem-solving model provided by the teacher will be accepted. Over a period of time and with a number of different examples, however, children are led through similar problem-solving sequences so that considerable repetition of these procedures may eventually occur.

At the beginning, the teacher initiates and directs the interactions. She or he prepares the environment for learning, presents new materials, and models the appropriate problem-solving procedures. However, as children become familiar with these, they may begin to manage some of their own learning encounters independently.

Many programs employ these question sequences (Figure 4.4, p. 47). Some, as we have seen, do so in conjunction with pattern repetitions. These tend to foster less independent encounters with the materials. Others do so in conjunction with less structured improvisations, encouraging greater independence.

Five programs rely almost exclusively on the use of these sequences: Lavatelli, Blank, Talkabout, Kamii and DeVries, and Focus on Meaning. All carefully describe the rationale for each question sequence and present a variety of examples of each problem-solving strategy and procedure. Lavatelli provides a more restricted set of sequences, based entirely on the manipulable materials which accompany the program. The others deal with a broader range of topics, using materials common to the classroom or easily constructed by the teacher.

This type of interaction represents an attempt to adapt what is known about the conditions of natural language acquisition to the needs of the child in the classroom. Thus, the emphasis is on the meaning of a statement rather than the form in which it is uttered. Although rote repetition of new forms may be required, this never comprises more than a small percentage of the instructional period. However, unlike the situation at home, teachers do attempt to prestructure the learning environment so that certain words will be elicited and, presumably, added to the child's repertoire.

The advantage in this kind of learning interaction lies in the fact that children are practicing language in situations where the focus is on solving a problem or communicating an idea rather than repeating a specific pattern. In the process children may be using language in a wider range of situations than would be available in a program which emphasized pattern repetition. The disadvantage is that there is no guarantee that each child will obtain a minimal amount of exposure to a specified set of utterances in each type of communication situation; what is said and when depends to a greater extent on a child's own needs and interests and the ingenuity of the teacher. The difference between this type of interaction and pattern repetition can be seen when we compare two lessons, each of which focuses on the development of classification skills. The first is from Lavatelli:

Find the Common Property of a Group of Objects

Distribute materials to the children.

T: "Today, each of you has a box of small toys. Let's put the toys on the table and see what you have. Tell me what you find, _____." (Ask each child in turn to name three of the toys. Supply vocabulary when needed. Allow ample time for the preliminary handling of objects.)

T: "Now I'd like you to find the toys that go together in some way. Let's start with the cup and saucer. Look carefully at all of the toys and see which ones you think might go with the cup and saucer. Put them on one of your pieces of cardboard."

T: (After children begin), "Tell me about your collection, _____. How do those objects go together?" (Ask each child in turn.)

T: (To the child who lines up the toys, or who puts things together on the basis of "belonging"; i.e., the dog eats out of the plate, so the plate "belongs with" the dog), "Could this object (spoon) belong with or go with the cup? Is it like the cup in some way? How? Which will you choose next?" (If the child rejects the classification, continue with the next step. If he recognizes and names the common property, praise him and continue.)

T: "Now put another piece of cardboard on the table, and this time let's put the dog on the cardboard. Look at the toys that are left and see if you can find some that are like the dog in some way, but a way that's different from your first collection. Put them on the new piece of cardboard." Repeat the directions carried out for the first collection of objects. Have the children make a third collection out of what is left.

T: "Do these (hammer, screwdriver, saw) go together in some way? How are they alike?" (Lavatelli [Teacher's Guide, classification, Set 5] p. 26)

Throughout, the children are asked to explain their groupings. The teacher's questions about the objects seem to have the double function of focusing attention on object attributes and helping children describe the similarities and differences that they notice. Although the objects seem to be related primarily in terms of function (cups, plates, and saucers; saws, hammers, and screwdrivers), the teacher is cautioned to accept other groupings if the child offers an appropriate explanation or rationale. Nor are children expected to couch their explanations in a particular kind of vocabulary or syntax; any wording that communicates the child's explanation seems to be acceptable. The emphasis, then, is on the production of explanations which fit the child's more or less spontaneous classifications, not on the learning of some predefined kind of classification scheme or on some specific language for communicating explanations.

By contrast, the second example from DISTAR is concerned entirely with the learning of a particular classification scheme and a particular kind of language:

We're going to learn a rule about plants.

a. Point to each plant and ask:
    What kind of plant is this?
    The children are to answer a tree, a bush, a flower.

b. Here's a rule about all plants. Listen.
    If it grows in the ground, it is a plant.
    Listen again.
    If it grows in the ground, it is a plant.
    Everybody, say the rule with me.
    Signal. Respond with the children.
    If it grows in the ground, it is a plant.

c. Again. Signal. Respond with the children.
    If it grows in the ground, it is a plant.
    Repeat *c* until all children's responses are firm.

d. All by yourselves. Say the rule about plants. Pause.
    Signal.
    If it grows in the ground, it is a plant.

e. Again. Signal.
    If it grows in the ground, it is a plant.

Repeat *e* until all children's responses are firm.

Now let's look at the objects on the next page. Turn the page quickly.

f. Point to the bush.

   Does this grow in the ground? Touch. *Yes.* **If it grows in the ground, it's a**
   _____ .

   Touch *plant*. A bush grows in the ground.
   So what do you know about a bush? Touch.
   It's a plant.

g. Again. What do you know about a bush?
   Touch. *It's a plant.*
   Repeat *g* until all children's responses are firm.

h. Point to the coat.
   Does this grow in the ground? Touch. *No.*
   A coat does not grow in the ground.
   So what do you know about a coat? Touch.
   It's not a plant.

i. Again. What do you know about a coat?
   Touch. *It's not a plant.*
   Repeat *i* until all children's responses are firm.

j. Point to the airplane.
   Does this grow in the ground? Touch. *No.*
   An airplane does not grow in the ground.
   So what do you know about an airplane?
   Touch. *It's not a plant.*

k. Again. What do you know about an airplane?
   Touch. *It's not a plant.*
   Repeat *k* until all children's responses are firm.

l. Point to the carrot.
   Does this grow in the ground? Touch. *Yes.*
   If it grows in the ground, it's a _____ .
   Touch. *plant*. A carrot grows in the ground. So what do you know about a
   carrot?
   Touch. *It's a plant.*

m. Again. What do you know about a carrot?
   Touch. *It's a plant.*
   Repeat *m* until all children's responses are firm.

n. Repeat *f* through *m* until all children's responses are firm. (DISTAR
   [Teacher's Materials Classification, Task 8] pp. 108-109)

In contrast with the Lavatelli lesson, the assumption here is that children need to learn a particular rule or verbal formula. It is unclear how much the rule-learning is expected to increase children's underlying classification skills, but the assumption seems to be that the children are already skilled at making a distinction between plants and non-plants; what they must learn is to express that knowledge in a certain way. By contrast, the Lavatelli materials seem to focus on acquisition of more fundamental classification skills rather than on a particular language for expressing them.

Single questions and spontaneous conversations

Several programs seem to rely on more spontaneous discussions or conversations. The teacher is not given a complicated instructional agenda but is reasonably free to accept all comments offered by a child. Language in such programs seems to have a self-expressive function: Children are encouraged to describe their reactions to materials, but these descriptions are not necessarily used as material for enacting problem-solving procedures or strategies. For example, children may be asked to name favorite foods and even to describe their taste. But in most cases, the program will not provide explicit instructions for helping children organize their observations more formally into food categories (e.g., meat, vegetables, dairy products) or categories of taste (e.g., sweet and sour). Programs of this type include Whispers, Bowmar, Concepts, and Kindle.

Improvisation and storytelling

Among activities with the least predetermined language are improvisation, dramatization, and storytelling, activities in which roles, intentions, and outcomes are (to some extent) set ahead of time, but in which the actual interactions and language are constructed spontaneously by the children.

In contrast to pattern repetition, this type of interaction places children in situations where they attempt to communicate rather than imitate a model; success is based on the functional adequacy of a communication, not on whether it matches a specific model, and in this sense it differs from what is expected under either pattern repetition or structured questioning. In its emphasis on the process of interaction, this type of activity also provides children with tasks that are more open-ended, in which the children are free to try a variety of different strategies and indeed to change the course of the learning encounter to suit their own needs. That is, a child has many more options if the task is to act out the resolution of a quarrel with another child than if it is to describe a picture. As a result, children must be concerned with communication strategies as well as syntax and vocabulary. They must adapt their message to the needs of others. Children must also take into account their purposes within the role and the dramatic situation. These are things which must be done in the course of many communication situations inside and ouside the classroom, but not usually in the teacher-dominated school lesson.

The required concern with communication strategies is an advantage with this type of learning interaction. Because the children are responsible for executing (and in sociodramatic play even selecting) an intent as well as an utterance, the learning situation mirrors most closely the communication situations which they are likely to encounter outside of school. In addition, learning situations can be structured to elicit syntactic structures which children need to practice. (For example, if a child is asked to undertake the role of a doctor, she may well have to persuade her reluctant patient to take medicine and, in the process, use words such as *if, because.*) Thus, a second advantage in this kind of approach is the chance for children to practice syntactic structures in a wide range of contexts—a strategy likely to lead to maximum transfer. The activities in Talk Reform provide good examples of how situations can be structured to elicit specific syntactic forms.

One disadvantage with this type of learning interaction is that it provides very little opportunity to introduce new vocabulary. Although teachers may focus attention on the names of certain objects by introducing them as props to be used during the dramatization, teachers have little opportunity to deal with new words once the dramatization is underway. Thus, a program which relies on improvised interaction should probably provide an opportunity for teachers to introduce vocabulary in another type of learning situation.

Eight programs emphasize improvisation and storytelling (Figure 4.4, p. 47). These seem to be of two types, depending on whether they also include the more highly structured question sequences or whether they emphasize more spontaneous discussion and conversation.

The properties of the four types of student-teacher interaction are summarized in Figure 4.5 (p. 54). As we can see from the chart, each interaction differs in terms of task requirements, functions of language, and the roles of teacher and student. In the pattern repetition interactions, the main task is to *imitate* exact language, and success is judged on the *form* of a child's statement—whether it matches the model in terms of syntax and vocabulary. In structured questioning, the main task is to learn certain problem-solving procedures, and while a minimum degree of intelligibility is required, success is primarily judged on the *meaning* of an utterance—does it represent an appropriate solution to the problem or a plausible way of describing a given event according to the expected strategies and procedures. In the single question/spontaneous conversations, the task is to comment on the materials provided by the teacher. Success depends on the extent to which the comment seems to reflect a sincere expression of the student's reactions. In the improvised interactions, the main task is to obtain a practical result by influencing the behavior of others. Success depends on such communication strategies as the ability to formulate a goal and organize a series of utterances during a dramatization so as to change another person's behavior.

Each type of interaction stresses a different aspect of language. At the same time, each also involves teachers and students in different types of roles. In the pattern repetition interactions, the teacher formulates the goals, initiates and manages the learning, and asks the questions. Students listen and formulate answers. In the structured questioning, the teacher sets the goals and to a large extent manages the course of the instruction, but both the teacher and the student are able to initiate learning encounters, ask questions, and formulate answers. The single question/spontaneous conversations and improvised interactions provide for the greatest

Figure 4.5

Description of Four Teacher/Student Interaction Types

Interaction type	Task requirements		Role of teacher (T) and student (S)				
	Task	*Criterion for success*	*Formulate goals and intentions*	*Initiate encounters*	*Change course of encounter*	*Ask questions*	*Answer questions*
Pattern repetition	imitate model	form of language	T	T	T	T	S
Structured question sequences	convey information	meaning	T	T	T/S	T/S	T/S
Single questions/ spontaneous conversations	express reactions	sincerity and relevance	T	T	T/S	T/S	T/S
Improvisations and storytelling	obtain practical result; influence another's behavior	communica- tion strategy	T/S	T/S	T/S	T/S	T/S

mutuality and sharing of roles. In the single question/spontaneous conversations, the teacher sets the topic, but the student is free to comment on any aspect. In the improvised interactions, teachers and students are both responsible for setting the topic and the course of the interaction.

In selecting a program, it is as important to consider the dominant type of interaction as it is to consider the subject matter, vocabulary, and syntax. As children participate in these early childhood programs they learn not only language, but also how to function in the role of a student. Therefore, in choosing a program it is important to consider the type of role which children will be expected to play as they continue in school. Thus, if children are expected to ask questions and initiate learning encounters (as, for example, in many discovery method curricula), then it is probably a good idea for them to have practice using the problem-solving procedures and strategies modeled in the structured questioning sequences. Most children, however, will be required to undertake many different student's roles in the course of their schooling—a situation which suggests that young children may need opportunities to participate in a variety of different interactions. If this is so, then the teacher would do well to choose materials which provide a range of interaction types or to use material from several programs that provide different types of interactions during the year.

Instructional management

In this section, we will briefly examine how these 30 programs are organized and how this may affect the way in which each is actually administered. We will examine three dimensions: the amount of presequencing provided by the materials, the type of evaluation provided, and the type of teacher's guide. Our purpose is to consider how much of the day-to-day curriculum is actually designed by the teacher and how much help in decision making is provided by the guide.

Presequencing

We have little validated information about how to sequence a language program for young children. We do not know whether sequencing really affects children's learning. But apart from the child, sequencing may be important for teachers, relieving them of the need to make day-to-day sequencing decisions—decisions which the teacher may neither have the time nor the training to make successfully alone.

Programs differ in the amount of presequencing. Some are entirely presequenced. The teacher knows in advance the content of any given lesson and when it should be presented. Programs of this sort are DISTAR, Peabody, Lavatelli, SWRL, Oral English, and BECP. Others have moderate amounts of presequenced material. There are sets of presequenced lessons on given topics, but these are to be used as the need arises.

Thus, teachers are responsible for diagnostic decisions, although once the diagnosis is made specific lesson plans can be followed. Programs of this sort include Whispers, Bomar, Yonemura, GOAL, Murphy and O'Donnell, Target, Wordworld, and Weikart. The remaining programs have very little presequenced material. In most cases, the topic to be studied is set in advance and a general course of action is outlined, but specific procedures will depend on decisions made by the teacher. For example, if the program involves discussion of a picture, the topic itself will be set by the picture's content and, to some extent, the vocabulary and syntax (particularly names of objects and attributes) will also be determined by the content. However, it is the teacher who will determine what is actually said and who does the talking. Thus, the teacher is responsible for making diagnostic decisions and decisions about the day-to-day structure of the curriculum.

Evaluation

The effectiveness of any program will depend to a large extent on the teacher's success in evaluating the progress of individual pupils. Two types of evaluation are important. First, teachers need to evaluate children's responses to particular questions during instruction so that they can correct the children, extend their responses, or indicate approval. This type of evaluation is discussed in the next section. Second, there is a more general kind of evaluation which assesses the child's overall language development, not with respect to the requirements of particular lessons, but in terms of the overall objectives of the total program. It is this type of evaluation which we will consider now.

As we can see from Figure 4.6, the majority of programs provide some sort of evaluation. Five provide general suggestions for assessment. Two (Whispers and Talkabout) offer only a sketchy indication of what the teacher should do. For example, in Talkabout, the teacher is told that evaluation can be accomplished by ". . . watching your kids and listening to them talk . . . noting their word increases and combinations from notes you've kept . . . forming individual and small-group check lists related to specific areas of language development such as word definition and vocabulary usage, sentence length (fluency or verbality), structure (syntax), order and complexity (sequencing)" (p. 32). Two others (Focus and Kamii and DeVries) provide extensive anecdotal comments and one, Intellectual Skills, provides special suggestions for helping teachers evaluate their own language as well as that of the children.

Four programs provide checklists to be used in evaluating children's progress through a block of activities, and seven provide the teacher with tests to be administered at the end of a group of lessons. For the most part, these are tied to the explicit goals of the programs. In the case of Goal, the evaluation is keyed to the language skills covered by the Illinois Test of Psycholinguistic Abilities assessment battery.

These tests and checklists seem to provide reasonable assessments of the skills emphasized in the lessons. In some cases, however, the evaluation procedures presuppose certain skills which are not covered in the lessons and which may be at least as complicated as the ones that are. For example, in Wordworld (Teacher's Guide, p. 66) the child must understand the difference between a line that is drawn under an object and one that appears above, in order to follow the test directions, despite the fact that

Figure 4.6

Types of Evaluation Procedures*

Program names	No special procedures	General suggestions	Checklist	Tests	Extensive detailed suggestions
Concepts	X				
Lavatelli	X				
Talk Reform	X				
Peabody	X				
ALG	X				
Kindle	X				
Bowmar	X				
Whispers		X			
Talkabout		X			
Focus		X			
Intellectual Skills		X			
Kamii and DeVries		X			
Goal			X		
Simonds			X		
Weikart			X		
Murphy and O'Donnell			X		
SELF				X	
SWRL				X	
Target				X	
Oral English				X	
Wordworld				X	
DISTAR				X	
BECP				X	
Yonemura					X
Minicourse					X
Blank					X
Talking and Learning					X

* These are descriptions of procedures for evaluating student's general progress with respect to a program's overall objectives or objectives relevant to a block of lessons. Evaluation of pupil responses within a specific lesson is described in the next section.

knowledge of these spatial terms is not being evaluated. In such cases, the teacher must be careful to distinguish between the child who has not learned the names of the objects being evaluated and the child who cannot comprehend the instructions.

Four programs provide detailed suggestions for extensive evaluation procedures. Blank provides detailed directions for evaluating both the child and the teacher's language in teacher-child interactions. Yonemura and Talking and Learning provide both tests and interview procedures for teachers to use. Minicourse is unique in that it was designed to be used as an inservice training vehicle for teachers anxious to improve their language curricula. It provides extensive suggestions for helping teachers monitor their own and the children's progress. In addition, it is the only program to suggest the use of pre- and post-curriculum evaluations of children's language as part of the evaluation.

Finally, we should mention Tough's *Listening to Children Talking* (1976), a guide for evaluating children's language that places particular emphasis on evaluations of language function. The detailed suggestions are appropriate for many kinds of language programs and could be used to supplement their evaluation procedures.

Type of teacher's guide

As soon as a teacher is required to make diagnostic or day-to-day curriculum decisions, the teacher's guide becomes important. It can provide the kind of rationale and detailed description of procedures which would help the teacher make good decisions or it can provide relatively little support. Guides differ in the amount and type of information provided, falling into four categories: extended explanations, script plus examples, script only, and topics plus suggested questions.

Extended explanations. The most specific guides provide what can be called extended explanations. These give detailed explanations of procedures, along with a rationale for each activity and examples of probable student responses. For each incorrect or inadequate response, the guide suggests an appropriate follow-up procedure, providing for branching within the overall sequencing of the program. As an example, consider this passage from Blank's program (italics [ours] indicate opportunities for branching):

> As tasks increase in complexity the child may become bewildered by the number of units with which he must deal. In such a case, the teacher may dissect the task into its various components so that the child can complete the problem in partial steps. The teacher can accomplish this goal *in one of two ways:*
>
> a. Isolate individual components by sequentially focusing the child on the various subunits forming the totality.
>   *Example:*
>   Teacher presents a group of blocks in a pattern and then says "Now you make the same pattern over here with these blocks."
>   **Child—_____.**

Teacher—"Show me the block at the bottom. Get one like it."
b. Introduce either a perceptual or verbal cue to restructure the situation so as to emphasize its significant characteristics.
Example:
Teacher—"Why do you think we couldn't get this sponge into the (small) cup and we could fit the marble?"
Child—"Because it's a sponge."
Teacher—"Okay, I'll cut this sponge into two.
Now it's still a sponge. Why does it go into the cup now?"

Both the above techniques share the need for the teacher to decide which parts should be emphasized and the order in which the totality should be dissected. The second technique, however, requires greater ingenuity since the totality is not composed of clearly recognizable units. As a result, skill is required to discern how a seemingly indivisible situation may be dissected and restructured (e.g., we are not accustomed to seeing sponges that are one inch in size). (Teaching Learning in the Preschool 1973, pp. 92.)

Programs of this type include: Kamii and DeVries, Minicourse, Focus, Blank, and Intellectual Skills.

Script plus examples. A second type of guide provides a script for the teacher plus examples of probable student responses. This type of guide is similar to the extended explanation, except that the teacher is given more explicit language to use. This type of guide provides the same opportunities for branching, as we can see from the following examples (italics [ours] indicate branching suggestions):

T: "Today, each of you has a box of small toys. Let's . . . see what you have. Tell me what you find. . ." (Ask each child in turn to name three of the toys. Supply vocabulary when needed.)
T: *(To the child who lines up the toys, or who puts things together on the basis of "belonging". . . .)* "Could this object (spoon) belong with or go with the cup? Is it like the cup in some way?" *(If the child rejects the classification, continue. . . . If he recognizes and names the common property, praise him and continue.)* (Early Childhood Curriculum, Teacher's Guide 1973, p. 26)

Programs which provide this type of guide include Lavatelli, Talking and Learning, and BECP.

Taken together, the extended explanation and the script plus examples are the most specific types of guides. If used with programs of moderate or low levels of presequencing, they can enable the teacher to take advantage of their flexibility without becoming disorganized, since a detailed rationale for making curriculum decisions is provided.

Script only. A third type of guide provides a script for the teacher, with few examples of probable student response. Thus, there is no provision for branching, although the procedures for the basic lesson are very specific. Programs with this type of guide include Oral English, Peabody, DISTAR, GOAL, SWRL, and Target.

The problem with this type of guide is that it seems to assume that children will respond according to the script; there are few examples of possible incorrect responses and almost no suggestions for alternative remedial teaching procedures. At best, the teacher is simply told to recycle the child through parts of the program.

Topics and suggested questions. A fourth type of guide provides a list of topics and some suggested questions but procedures are not described in step-by-step detail. For example:

Making Pudding

"Often overlooked are the many chances to label ingredients and utensils while using them. The *milk,* the *pudding powder,* the *cup,* the *spoon,* and the *bowl* should become part of the dialogue between you and the child. Begin with frequent statements, questions, and restatements:

'Let's pour the pudding powder into the bowl now, Nilda.' Then when done: 'What did you just do, Nilda? Tell Ronnie so he can do it, too.'

And so with each of the action words. Once the statement pattern and words are heard, they can be used and reused by the children.

There's really lots more to cooking than the social and conceptual learnings we tend to use it for. And even the concepts (in this instance, of textural and color changes caused by adding milk to the powder) can be productive of language. Frame questions around them, using the labels of the ingredients:

'What happens to the color of the pudding powder when we pour in milk?' 'What's happening to the pudding as we beat it?' (Talkabout, Vol. 2 1976, pp. 157-158)

And from another program:

"Let Me See You Try"

Things to talk about: What are some of the things that the children in the story can do? Which of these things have you done? What are some other things you can try? Which do you enjoy most? (Bowmar, Teacher's Guide 1968, p. 16)

Programs with this type of guide include Bowmar, ALG, Weikart, Yonemura, Talk Reform, Concepts, Kindle, SELF, Whispers, and Talkabout.

In cases where the program is presequenced and where the teacher makes relatively few curriculum decisions, this type of guide is almost as adequate as a complete script. However, where the teacher alone is required to do some of the sequencing (as, for example, in the case of Weikart, Yonemura, Talk Reform, and ALG), this type of guide may well be inadequate since it does not provide sufficient rationale for making day-to-day curriculum decisions.

Concluding notes and recommendations

It seems important to consider some of the information presented in the preceding sections as it pertains to the following questions: the need for dialect training; the role of overt practice in language education; the type of teacher characteristics demanded by various kinds of learning interactions; the role of materials for the child; and the role of the school and community in selecting a language curriculum.

Dialect training

Some programs, designed for speakers of nonstandard dialects, attempt to teach children to use standard English or what is sometimes called a school dialect. There are some very good reasons why parents from nonstandard-English speech communities may wish their children to learn standard English. However, there is one thing that learning standard English cannot do, and we must emphasize this fact: Functionally, as a means of communication and as support for cognitive behavior, the learning of standard English is of no intrinsic advantage. There is no evidence indicating that any dialect is superior to any other as a tool for thinking or for the communication of ideas. This is not to say that all languages are the same. A thought will be expressed in different ways in different language systems. But functionally, each system is equivalent. Therefore, we cannot base a language curriculum on the notion that one language or dialect should be taught because it enables children to think more clearly or have better ideas. Some programs do make this claim.

Another misconception is that nonstandard dialects do not contain the means for expressing a full range of grammatical relationships; that they are, in some way, less flexible than standard dialect. This misconception probably results from the way in which some educators approach the notion of dialect. What they seem to do is attempt to match a nonstandard dialect against standard English and—when a difference occurs—they seem to assume that the difference indicates a deficiency in the nonstandard forms. That is, they treat the points of difference as if they represented weaknesses in the nonstandard dialect. As a result, the educators feel they can justifiably describe a dialect as not having a past perfect tense or a copulative or whatever. Of course, such a description is completely absurd. Nonstandard dialects simply follow different rules. It is not our purpose to describe such rules here; the interested reader can begin by referring to *English in Black and White* (Burlings 1973).

Most programs which focus on syntax (Figure 4.2, p. 39) rest to a greater or lesser extent on these questionable assumptions. The results need not necessarily be inadequate. However, there are two real dangers. First, the practice of isolated syntax fragments may seem like meaningless school work to children who may very well fail to understand how the lessons relate to their own language system or even to the system of standard English which they have certainly become acquainted with—if not in school, then through television. This, in turn, may lead them to think that what is taught in school may be nonfunctional or inapplicable to real life. This is hardly the result we have in mind when we talk about helping children acquire basic communication tools. Second, the underlying assumption may affect teacher attitudes toward children. Teachers must understand that dialect has nothing whatsoever to do with the level of a child's mental development or ability to learn in school.

If dialect-training is to be undertaken, the teacher must deal with the child's existing dialect as well as the new one. Children are likely to assume that if language change is required, then the existing language must be considered in some way deficient. This in turn may lead children to feel ashamed of their own home dialect or to reject the new one. The process must be undertaken with considerable tact. At the very least, programs should provide the teacher with some information about the nonstandard dialects, particularly some means of identifying areas where speakers of standard and nonstandard dialects are likely to misunderstand each other. (For a start, each teacher's guide should include at least a glossary of syntactic structures in their various nonstandard and standard forms and also, when necessary, information about phonological variations which may affect interpretation of meaning.) Additionally, there should be concrete suggestions for helping both the teacher and the children maintain respect for and interest in the home dialect.

It is possible to imagine a dialect training program which treats both dialects with respect and, in addition, treats each dialect as the intact system which, in fact, it is. Such programs would develop children's awareness of language and dialects as alternative coding systems as well as provide practice switching between the two. Activities could include some of the following: listening to tapes of the same story told in each dialect; listening to tapes of stories in which each character speaks a different dialect; providing dialogue for puppets, each of which speaks a different dialect; role-playing situations in which the characters speak with different dialects; translating the same message from one dialect to another; inventing a simple dialect or coding system. At the very least, this kind of approach, if used in conjunction with some of the other available programs, would help children maintain respect for their home dialect while learning to communicate in a second dialect, because the dialects are treated as separate, equivalent systems.

The role of overt practice

There is some evidence that children in language programs learn what they actually practice. Therefore, if we want to change what children say, our best strategy is to make sure that they have a chance to speak the desired words and structures. In choosing a program, it is especially important to consider what children will actually be required to say and to make sure that all have an opportunity to practice using the desired language. Programs in which children listen or act without speaking while the teacher does most of the talking, and programs in which the teacher's language is more elaborate than that required of the children may prove inadequate. Although the language that children hear is obviously important, it is the language that they actually use which seems to make a change in their speaking behavior.

The simplest way to insure that all children participate is to provide experiences with a high degree of uniformity and to presequence the curriculum. In this way, all teachers will be doing roughly the same thing and all children will be required to respond in roughly the same way. The drawback to this type of program is that there is little room for individualization (apart from minor deviations in the way in which standard lessons are paced). Teachers are not encouraged to change the curriculum to suit individual needs and children are often required to waste their time practicing language which they already know how to use. A better solution is to select a program which has low or moderate presequencing and uniformity plus an adequately detailed teacher's guide. However, many teachers will need more than the printed page (no matter how well written) to guide them in making day-to-day decisions. On-site supervision is the ideal solution, but this is expensive, and sufficient personnel may simply not be available. Short of this, publishers might be encouraged to produce films, videotapes, filmstrips, and tape recordings to help less experienced teachers become more familiar with the way in which good decisions are made. One important step in this direction is Minicourse which is explicitly designed to provide inservice training in using a language curriculum. Listening to Children represents another useful step, in that it provides the teacher with extensive suggestions for evaluating children's language.

The role of children's materials

Programs which include children's materials are substantially more expensive than those which provide only a guide for the teacher and yet, as we have seen, the latter (which rely on teacher-made materials or materials generally available in any preschool classroom) can be at least as comprehensive and detailed (Kamii and DeVries, Blank, Focus on Meaning, and Target). In many cases, teachers in reasonably well-stocked early childhood classrooms may find it preferable to purchase one or two of these excellent guide books. At the very least, the teacher will want to think carefully before purchasing programs with materials that might be somewhat similar to those already in the classroom or which might be made by the teacher. In almost every curriculum category, the two types of programs exist. For example, syntactic programs include DISTAR and Peabody (with children's materials) as well as Target and Yonemura (without).

Teacher characteristics

In choosing a program, it is important to keep in mind the characteristics of the teachers who will be using it, and particularly their preferred ways of interacting with children. Programs do make different kinds of demands, depending on the type of learning interaction (see Figure 4.4, pp. 47).

Programs based on pattern repetition interactions require that teachers hold the children's attention primarily with their voices. The children are not free to move around; there is little for them to do except listen and talk. In this kind of situation, the teacher has to be a good performer. Everything will depend on the teacher's ability to hold the children's attention for periods lasting up to 20 or even 30 minutes.

While programs based on instructional dialogue and on improvised interactions may require somewhat similar behavior (especially if the program relies heavily on teacher-led discussion), attention is not focused entirely on the teacher for long periods of time. Children are encouraged to interact with each other and develop new ideas on their own. Rather than holding children's attention, the teacher may be more concerned with figuring out children's meanings, interpreting their utterances to others, and helping them expand their ideas. The teacher will probably spend less time performing in front of the group and more time arranging the class environment or engaging in brief conversations with a few children who are attempting to solve a given problem or to put their experiences into words. The teacher will have to make a lot more on-the-spot curriculum decisions in terms of both goals and procedures.

The roles of the school and community

In choosing a program, it is important to consider both the demands of later schooling as well as the child's present and future role within the community. For this, the educator simply may not be as well informed as parents and other community adults. This is especially true if the educator and the child come from different language communities or ethnic groups. Therefore, it seems essential that parents be made aware of the curriculum options and their implications when a language program is to be selected. Their opinions should be given considerable weight when the actual choice is made, for language is a most delicate and personal matter—involving a person's cultural heritage, the family which transmits that heritage, and the very self which a person seeks to express. Language can serve to enrich a person's existing capacity for verbal communication or it can lead a person ultimately to feel ashamed and unsure of her or his ability to communicate. We can avoid such potentially disastrous results if we take time to consider the implications of what children will be asked to do and if, above all, we take time to consult with members of the child's own community.

Programs for parents

A few materials for parents have also recently appeared on the market. Three typical ones are *Learning Language at Home, Teach Your Child to Talk,* and *200 Ways to Help Children Learn While You're at It* (see Figure 4.1, pp. 35-36). *Learning Language at Home* seems to be intended for use with language-handicapped children, although the guide suggests that it can be used with normal children. The program involves 30-40 minute daily tutoring sessions in which parent and child engage in structured question sequences and occasional improvisations. The lessons are highly sequenced, the procedures are fairly explicit, and the materials would probably be readily available in most middle-class homes. Since the material in the lessons is similar to that found in many preschool programs, it would seem unnecessary for the normal child, attending nursery school, to participate in this type of program at home. For the language handicapped, however, these lessons may be appropriate.

Despite its somewhat dubious title, *Teach Your Child to Talk* is a low-keyed, sensitive, and informative book for parents about language development.

It stresses the parent's role in modeling language for the child but cautions parents against rejecting or correcting the immaturities which naturally occur in the speech of young children. It provides a series of realistic milestone tables so that parents can be aware of children's progress and can, in the case of delayed development, seek professional help. Suggestions for fostering language development are simple and could be accomplished in the course of usual parent-child interactions; no special lesson times are specified. Many ethnic groups are represented in the pictures and the text refers to objects and customs from a variety of cultural and racial groups. The author adopts a generally reassuring tone. He is not condescending to parents, and the text is clear, easy to read, and filled with very practical advice. Its realistic picture of language development would be informative to teachers and other staff members as well as parents.

Two Hundred Ways to Help Children Learn While You're at It is a book of activities that parents can use to foster intellectual development, about one-third of which are specifically aimed at language development. The suggestions are practical and, as the title suggests, easily integrated into everyday household events. It does not attempt to provide the basic developmental information of a book such as *Teach Your Child to Talk,* but it does provide a wider range of specific activities. Indeed, the two books seem to complement each other—the one providing considerable basic information, and the other a greater number of engaging activities.

References

Burlings, R. *English in Black and White.* New York: Holt, Rinehart & Winston, 1973.
Hohmann, H.; Banet, B.; and Weikart, D. P. *Young Children in Action: A Manual for Preschool Educators.* Ypsilanti, Mich.: High/Scope, 1979.
Tough, J. *Listening to Children Talking.* London: Ward Lock Educational, 1976.

Figure 4.7

Publishers for these kits may be found in Figure 4.1 (pp. 35-36).

I. Description of Materials

Blank. *Teaching Learning in the Preschool*
Author(s): Blank
Content: Mathematical/logical reasoning, cognitive code, and vocabulary
Interaction: Structured questioning sequences, low presequencing, extended explanation
Curriculum manual: 324 pp.; contains suggested activities and extended examples of teacher-child dialogue

Scheduled use: One-to-one tutorial sessions; 15 to 20 minutes per day
Price: $6.95.

Focus. *Focus on Meaning*
Author(s): Tough
Content: Mathematical/logical reasoning, social reasoning
Interaction: Structured questioning sequences, low presequencing, extended expla-
    nation
Curriculum manual: 127 pp.; focus on different types of teacher questions and the
    corresponding "mental demands" which they place on the child to whom they
    are directed
Scheduled use: Individual child and teacher, small groups, integrated into school day
Price: $6.50.

Intellectual Skills. *Intellectual Skills and Language*
Author(s): Hobson and McCauley
Content: Equal emphasis on cognitive code, vocabulary, and mathematical/logical
    reasoning; less emphasis on aesthetic uses, metalinguistic awareness, and social
    reasoning
Interaction: Single question, improvisation and storytelling, low presequencing, ex-
    tended explanation
Curriculum manual: 90 pp.; contains extended examples of teacher-child dialogue
Scheduled use: Small and large group, integrated into school day
Price: $3.00.

Kamii and DeVries. *Physical Knowledge in Preschool Education*
Author(s): Kamii and DeVries
Content: Greatest emphasis on mathematical/logical reasoning, less on social rea-
    soning
Interaction: Structured questioning sequences, low presequencing, extended expla-
    nation
Curriculum manual: 321 pp.; contains Piaget's theory of constructivism as applied to
    early childhood education, suggestions for specific activities, and examples of
    extended teacher-child dialogues around certain of the suggested activities
Scheduled use: Small and large groups, integrated into school day
Price: $12.95.

Minicourse. *Developing Children's Oral Language*
Author(s): Ward and Kelley
Content: Mathematical/logical reasoning, equal emphasis on syntactic learning and
    cognitive code, less emphasis on vocabulary and metalinguistic awareness
Interaction: Pattern repetition and structured questioning sequences, low pre-
    sequencing, extended explanation
Curriculum manual: 191 pp.; divided into five instructional sequences: teacher be-
    haviors for expanding language and thought, teacher behaviors for establishing
    language patterns, teaching the use of language to describe position, teaching the

use of language to describe and classify objects, and teaching the use of language to describe and identify action; also includes a series of pictures to be used to assess use of positional, descriptive, and action words (instructional and model lesson films for teacher viewing are also available)
Scheduled use: Small groups, unclear if integrated into school day or not—no scheduled time specified
Price: Purchase—$1,399.00. Rental—(6 weeks) $206.75. Teacher's handbook—$2.25. Coordinator's handbook—$3.80.

Simonds. *Language Skills for the Young Child*
Author(s): Simonds
Content: Equal emphasis on mathematical/logical reasoning, communicative functions, and aesthetic functions, less on metalinguistic awareness, cognitive code, and social reasoning
Interaction: Single questions and improvisation and storytelling, low presequencing, essay
Curriculum manual: 77 pp.
Scheduled use: Individual child and teacher and small groups, integrated into school day
Price: $4.00.

Talk Reform. *Talk Reform*
Author(s): Gahagan and Gahagan
Content: Greatest emphasis on communicative functions, syntactic learning, and vocabulary, less on mathematical/logical reasoning, social reasoning, cognitive code, and metalinguistic awareness
Interaction: Spontaneous discussion, improvisation and storytelling, low presequencing, topics and suggested questions
Curriculum manual: Chapter outlining curriculum; 34 pp.
Scheduled use: Small and large groups, 20 minutes per day, full year
Price: $5.95.

Talkabout. *Talkabout*
Author(s): Pasamanick
Content: Equal emphasis on cognitive code, vocabulary, and mathematical/logical reasoning, less on metalinguistic awareness and aesthetic functions
Interaction: Structured questioning sequences, low presequencing, topics and suggested questions
Curriculum manual: 2 volumes (each 326 pp.)
Scheduled use: Individual child and teacher, small and large groups, integrated into school day
Price: $19.95.

Talking and Learning. *Talking and Learning*
Author(s): Tough
Content: (Varies depending on where child is in the development of her or his use of English), initially: greatest focus on syntactic learning, vocabulary, and com-

municative functions, later: emphasis on mathematical/logical reasoning

Interaction: Pattern repetition and structured questioning sequences, high pre-sequencing, scripts plus examples

Curriculum manual: 316 pp.

Scheduled use: Individual child and teacher and small groups, integrated into school day

Price: Approximately $6.00.

Target. *Target on Language Grammar Program*
Author(s): Novakovich, Smith, and Teegarden
Content: Syntactic learning, cognitive code, and vocabulary
Interaction: Pattern repetition, moderate presequencing, script only
Curriculum manual: 73 pp.
Scheduled use: Individual child and teacher and small group, unspecified length of time, option for integrating it into regular curriculum
Price: $5.00.

Weikart. *The Cognitively Oriented Curriculum*
Author(s): Weikart, Rogers, Adcock, and McClelland
Content: Equal emphasis on mathematical/logical reasoning and cognitive code
Interaction: Structured questioning sequences, spontaneous discussion, and improvisation and storytelling, moderate presequencing, topics and suggested questions
Curriculum manual: 196 pp. (list of materials needed, sample lesson plans, and index)
Scheduled use: Small and large groups, integrated into school day
Price: $4.50.

Yonemura. *Developing Language Programs for Young Disadvantaged Children*
Author(s): Yonemura
Content: Syntactic learning, vocabulary
Interaction: Pattern repetition, moderate presequencing, topic and suggested questions
Curriculum manual: 81 pp.
Scheduled use: 10-20 minutes per day, full year
Price: $11.50.

II. Children's and Teacher's Materials

These programs include materials for children, along with curriculum guides for the teacher.

ALG. *Amazing Life Games*
Author(s): Young
Content: Mathematical/logical reasoning, less emphasis on cognitive code, vocabulary, and metalinguistic awareness

Interaction: Structured questioning sequences and improvisation and storytelling, low presequencing, topics and suggested questions

Children's materials: 5 films, 3 Personal Record Books (books which the child puts together and creates "through recording his reactions to the words inside and around him"), 2 Picture Posters to stimulate storytelling, 4 wordless books (these provide instructions in how to construct things; the child reads the books by interpreting the pictures)

Teacher's materials: File box with 201 activity cards (front of card describes the activity, back of card does two things: first, it shows how the instructions on the front relate to one or more of the five subject areas—social studies, the arts, communication skills, science, and math—and second, it offers a rationale which describes how the activity might be expected to affect the development of children). Also included in the file box are a set of blank activity cards for teachers to use to add their own ideas to the file, a section called "Other Resources" for teachers to make note of the games, books, records, and films they find most useful, and the "Do It Myself File" which contains instructions for helping teachers to make or build some of the games or other devices which are mentioned on the activity cards.

Teacher's guide: 33 pp. containing general suggestions for use of each of the components of the program

Scheduled use: Individual child and teacher and small groups, integrated into school day

Price: $525.00.

BECP. *Bilingual Early Childhood Program*
Author(s): Nedler

Content: Equal emphasis on mathematical/logical reasoning, cognitive code, and vocabulary, less on syntactic learning, metalinguistic awareness, and social reasoning

Interaction: Single questions, spontaneous discussions, improvisation and storytelling, high presequencing, script plus examples

Children's materials: 2 filmstrips, 20 color cards, colored squares, drawings and photographs, 9 records

Teacher's materials: Preservice manual (3 volumes), inservice manual (2 volumes), curriculum manuals (6 English, 6 Spanish), home activities for parents (manual), Paso a Paso manual, and parent involvement component (each manual is 200 to 300 pp.), 180 die cut sheets, spirit masters, and transparencies

Scheduled use: Small groups, 10 to 20 minutes per lesson, not more than 4 lessons per day

Price: List—$826.68 and net—$620.00.

Bowmar. *Bowmar Early Childhood Series*
Author(s): Jaynes, Woodbridge, Curry, and Crume

Content: Greatest emphasis on social reasoning, less on mathematical/logical reasoning and vocabulary

Interaction: Single questions, moderate presequencing, topic and suggested questions

Children's materials: 72 color photographs in 3 sets; 30 related storybooks in 3 sets; 30 records (side 1: narrator reads story, side 2: narrator reads story again, asks questions, and sings related song)
Teacher's material: 35 page guide to the storybooks and posters, 68 page guide to the social science implications of the storybooks, questions printed on backs of posters
Scheduled use: Small and large groups, time unspecified
Price: $390.00.

Concepts. *Beginning Concepts I and II*
Author(s): Morris, Hoban, Mully, Davis, Simon, and Carson
Content: Greatest emphasis on cognitive code, less on mathematical/logical reasoning and social reasoning
Interaction: Spontaneous discussion, low presequencing, topics and suggested questions
Children's materials: 5 filmstrips for each unit, 5 foldout books of pictures for each unit, 5 packages of minibooks (total 170) for each unit
Teacher's materials: 1 teacher's guide (63 pp.) for each unit
Scheduled use: Could be used with small or large groups, time unspecified
Price: $67.50 for records, $77.50 for cassettes for each unit.

DISTAR. *DISTAR Language 1*
Author(s): Engelmann and Osborn
Content: Greatest emphasis on syntactic learning, less on cognitive code and mathematical/logical reasoning
Interaction: Pattern repetition and structured questioning sequences, high presequencing, script only
Children's materials: Three take-home books
Teacher's materials: Five teacher presentation books with scripts for lesson plans, one teacher's guide, one storybook, with 23 stories
Scheduled use: Half hour per day, 160 daily lessons
Price: List: Teacher Kit—$186.67, set of three take-home books for one student— $4.34; School: Teacher Kit—$140.00, take-home books—$3.25.

GOAL. *Goal Program: Language Development*
Author(s): Karnes
Content: Equal emphasis on mathematical/logical reasoning, cognitive code, and vocabulary, some emphasis on communicative functions, metalinguistic awareness, aesthetic uses, and social meaning
Interaction: Pattern repetition and structured questioning sequences, moderate presequencing, script only
Children's materials: Picture Cards (8 sets of 42 each—family, home, foods, things together, opposites, picture dominoes, alikes, and everyday objects; Situation Pictures (impossible pictures—8, action pictures—16, how we feel pictures—6, nursery rhyme pictures—6), Templates and Posters (12 each), Animal Puzzles—6, Patterns and Pieces—3 puppets included, Spin and Find Games (8 overlays: singular and plural objects, community helpers, animals, family mem-

bers, the home, fruits, opposite objects, things that go together), Scenes Around Us (12 murals: farm, city, grocery store, school room, department store, playground, winter, summer, spring, fall, animals in the zoo, boys and girls)

Teacher's materials: Teacher's guide—30 pp., model lesson plan cards (337): (auditory reception, visual reception, verbal expression, manual expression, auditory association, visual association, auditory sequential memory, auditory closure, grammatic closure, and visual closure)

Scheduled use: Small groups (5 to 8 children), 20 to 30 minutes per day for a half-day program, 40 to 60 minutes per day for a full-day program

Price: $130.00.

Kindle. *"How Can I Tell?" (Kindle V)*
Content: Social reasoning and vocabulary
Interaction: Spontaneous discussion, low presequencing, topic and suggested questions
Children's materials: 5 filmstrips and 5 LP records
Teacher's materials: Teacher's guide—45 pp.
Scheduled use: Not specified
Price: $59.50 with records. $69.50 with cassettes.

Kindle. *"How Do I Learn?" (Kindle II)*
Content: Metacognitive awareness (sections attempting to develop the child's awareness of the psychological processes of remembering, forgetting, planning, and "figuring things out"), mathematical/logical reasoning, and social reasoning
Interaction: Spontaneous discussion, low presequencing, topic and suggested questions
Children's materials: 5 filmstrips and 5 LP records
Teacher's materials: Teacher's guide—45 pp.
Scheduled use: Unspecified
Price: $59.50 with records. $69.50 with cassettes.

Lavatelli. *Early Childhood Curriculum*
Author(s): Lavatelli
Content: Greatest emphasis on mathematical/logical reasoning, less on cognitive code.
Interaction: Structured questioning sequences, high presequencing, script plus examples
Children's materials: 21 sets of miniature toys and objects, 1 set per unit (enough materials for six children to use at a time)
Teacher's materials: 163 pp.; theoretical text describing Piaget's theory and its relationship to the preschool curriculum, 93 pp. teacher's guide providing directions for use of the materials
Scheduled use: Small groups, 10 minutes initially, increasing in duration as children's attention spans increase
Price: $323.45.

Murphy and O'Donnell. *Developing Oral Language with Young Children*
Author(s): Murphy and O'Donnell
Content: Greatest emphasis on vocabulary, less on cognitive code, metalinguistic
   awareness, mathematical/logical reasoning, and social reasoning
Interaction: (not included in chart), moderate presequencing (not included in text)
Children's materials: 6 workbooks (speech, listening, self-image, vocabulary and per-
   ception, number concepts, motor activities, and fun and games)
Teacher's materials: Introductions to children's books and parts of the children's
   books
Scheduled use: Not specified; time not specified (not to exceed 15 minutes per book)
Price: $11.50.

Oral English. *Oral English*
Author(s): Thomas and Allen
Content: Syntactic learning, cognitive code, and vocabulary
Interaction: Pattern repetition, high presequencing, script only
Children's materials: Workbook—128 pp.
Teacher's materials: Teacher's manual—182 pp., Language Development Cards
   (pictures), 3 wall charts, 1 pocket chart (for weather)
Scheduled use: Small or large groups, time unspecified, program designed to be
   finished in first half of year
Price: List prices: Language Skills Text—$2.52, Teacher's Manual—$2.52, Lan-
   guage Development Cards, Group A—$113.00, Language Development Cards,
   Group B—$44.80, Pocket Chart and Wall Chart—$51.00. Net delivered prices:
   Language Skills Text—$1.89, Teacher's Manual—$1.89, Language Development
   Cards, Group A—$84.75, Language Development Cards, Group B—$33.60,
   Pocket Chart and Wall Chart—$38.25.

Peabody. *Peabody Language Development Kit*
Author(s): Dunn, Horton, and Smith
Content: Greatest emphasis on syntactic learning and mathematical/logical reasoning, much less emphasis on cognitive code, general vocabulary, communicative
   functions, aesthetic functions, metalinguistic awareness, and social reasoning
Interaction: Pattern repetition and single questions, high presequencing, script only
Children's materials: 422 picture cards, 6 posters, 10 records, 3 puppets, 21 models of
   fruit and vegetables, xylophone, boy and girl mannequins and vinyl clothing,
   unassembled mannequin (to teach names of parts of the body), 45 magnetic
   geometric shapes, 240 plastic chips (used to reward learning)
Teacher's materials: 399 page guide (lessons are not indexed and there is no table of
   contents, the teacher will thus have difficulty altering any of the lesson sequences
   to suit her needs)
Scheduled use: Small or large groups, two 20 minute periods per day, 180 days
Price: $192.00.

SELF. *SELF*
Author(s): Manolakes and Scian

Content: Greatest emphasis on social reasoning, less on mathematical/logical reasoning, vocabulary, communicative functions, and metalinguistic awareness

Interaction: Spontaneous discussion and improvisation and storytelling, low presequencing, topics and suggested questions

Children's materials: Self-Told Tales (3 sets of 36 picture books), Self Packs (102 picture cards), Self Pads (40 each of 48 different experience sheets), Self Sounds (10 records), Self Search (large illustration of sounds), Gabby Puppets (3), Together (40 each of 24 different leaflets for parents)

Teacher's materials: Teacher Resource Manuals (6), total pages—115

Scheduled use: Small groups, 20 minutes per day, 3 times per week

Price: $198.00.

SWRL. *Communication Skills Program: Expressive Language*

Author(s): Southwest Regional Laboratories

Content: Greatest emphasis on communicative functions (verbal and nonverbal), less on social reasoning and mathematical/logical reasoning

Interaction: Spontaneous discussion and improvisation and storytelling, high presequencing, script only

Children's materials: Dialogue Sentence Sheets, Tongue Twister Sheets, and Puppet Sheets

Teacher's materials: Activities and Materials Guide—Block 1 (7 pp.), Activities and Materials Guide—Block 2 (7 pp.), Program Guide: Expressive Language—Blocks 1 to 8 (15 pp.), teacher procedure cards containing specific directions for conducting the instructional activities, the criterion exercise, and the supplementary instruction for each unit; criterion exercises; activity posters providing illustrations of people and story characters in situations which pupils will pantomime and improvise; audio tapes—provide pupils with performance models such as appropriate use of vocal expression to convey mood or personality of a character

Scheduled use: Small groups, 20 minutes per session, 3 sessions suggested per week

Price: $43.70.

Whispers. *Whispers*

Author(s): Markavitch

Content: Equal emphasis on cognitive code and mathematical/logical reasoning, less on metalinguistic awareness

Interaction: Single questions, moderate presequencing, topics and suggested questions

Children's materials: Worksheets

Teacher's materials: Teacher's activity guide—123 pp. (The guide is organized into sections, one for each unit objective. Three elements are included in each section: statement of learning objective, a listing of developmental activities arranged in order from simplest to most difficult, and guidelines for determining mastery of objective. There are three major sections to the curriculum: vocabulary development, usage and syntax, and symbolization.); individual pupil record cards, "Pipermaster"—contains duplicating masters of worksheets designed to develop and provide practice on specific objectives

Scheduled use: Small groups, 20 minutes per day, 3 times per week
Price: $32.00.

Wordworld. *Wordworld*
Author(s): Lane, Sucher, and McCay
Content: Greatest emphasis on vocabulary, less on cognitive code and metalinguistic awareness
Interaction: Pattern repetition, moderate presequencing, topics and suggested questions in Extended Activities Section
Children's materials: 19 cassette tapes, 29 booklets (8 pp. each), 9 Star/Poster pages (evaluation and take-home sheets)
Teacher's materials: Teacher's handbook—104 pp., which includes class profile chart, duplicating masters: 3 for review of units 1 and 2, 9 Spanish/English letters to parents
Scheduled use: Individual child, 9-16 minutes per taped lesson
Price: List: tape set—$192.40, pupil's materials (set of 38 per pupil)—$7.96, teacher's handbook—$4.36, duplicating masters—$5.28. Net delivered: tape set—$144.30, pupil's materials—$5.97, teacher's handbook—$3.27, and duplicating masters—$3.96.

III. Parent's Materials

Learning Language at Home
Author(s): Karnes
Children's materials: None
Parent's materials: Guide—55 pp. (pp. 20-51 are a Record of Progress form), box of 200 activity cards
Scheduled use: Specific lessons—not more than 30-40 minutes per day, suggestions for other activities and general interaction patterns to be used throughout the day
Price: $130.00.

Teach Your Child To Talk
Author(s): Pushaw
Children's materials: None
Parent's materials: Text—*Teach Your Child to Talk*—248 pp.
Materials for Parents Through Workshops: Workshop Manual (for workshop leader)—29 pp., 278 color slides, 30 taped segments, color film
Price: Complete kit with film—$295.00, kit without film—$175.00, parent handbook—$2.25.

200 Ways to Help Your Child Learn While You're at It
Author(s): Braun
Children's materials: None

Parent's materials: Text
Scheduled use: Integrated into child's day at home
Price: $9.95.

Jean Berko Gleason

5.
An Experimental Approach to Improving Children's Communicative Ability

Some observers, notably Bernstein (1972), stated that working-class children use a different style when they are asked to describe pictures than do middle-class children. In fact, there seem to be overall style differences that characterize the speech of these two different social groups in England. The speech of the lower-income group Bernstein referred to as *restricted code:* it is rather as if the speakers are always talking to people who know the pictures well. A picture of a boy kicking a football through a window might be described as "He's broken it." The speech is restricted in the sense that it contains pronouns rather than nouns, few adverbs and adjectives, a minimum of dependent clauses, and is generally not very informative. By contrast, the descriptions used by middle-class children and the general speech of the middle-class in England is called *elaborated code*. The speaker takes less for granted, and tells more: uses more nouns, adjectives, and adverbs, and a greater variety of syntactic forms. Because these differences can be noted in speech, there is some question as to whether elaborated and restricted codes represent similarly elaborated and restricted underlying thought processes. It has been suggested that this is so, and that the speaker of restricted code is permanently locked into a kind of thought that makes higher-order abstract concepts unattainable to the speaker. I believe that the sociolinguistic experiment I conducted with Kay Atkinson King and Barbara Mandelkorn shows that this is not so.

Our experiment was conducted with 16 preschool children at a Cambridge, Massachusetts nursery school. Basically, what we wanted to deter-

Conducted at the Harvard School of Education in 1969-1970 under OEO Research Contract B-994809 to Arthur McCaffrey.

77

mine was whether or not nursery school children of different backgrounds and different abilities would show different kinds of ability or style in describing pictures, and whether or not those who seemed least able to produce a good description could be taught to use a different style or to produce a better description. In Bernstein's terms, would we find restricted code users and elaborated code users? Could the restricted code users be taught to use elaborated code, or was their style already frozen at the age of four? We wanted first to assess the communicative ability of the children, and then see if training sessions or games centered directly on picture describing could improve the descriptions later used by those children that we selected to be in the training group.

The ability to describe something so that someone else can recognize it is a skill that is needed to progress in school. For instance, when my daughter Cindy was in the third grade, one of her homework assignments was to write a composition describing something, but not telling what it is. She wrote: "It is little and round; it is green. It smells sower [*sic*] and it's hard." If she had also said, "It grows on a tree," I think I would have recognized the crab apple she was talking about, however, it was not a bad description. Because narrative, descriptive written langauge does not come easily at the age of seven, when children first start to get homework assignments, it seems likely that a foundation must be laid at an earlier age, and in spoken language. You have to assume that before children can write descriptions at the age of seven, they have to be able to say them aloud at six or five or four.

The four-year-olds we worked with were in a nursery school with a population of children from varied backgrounds. One-half of our sample was from a low-income background and one-half was from a middle-income background. The occupations of the children's parents ranged from unskilled laborer to college professor.

In deciding which children were good at describing, we used a variety of measures. We did not assume, a priori, that social class would predict whether or not a child had high verbal skill. Our basic way of judging the children's ability was through a variation of a standard communication experiment. We saw the children in pairs that the teacher had selected on the basis of mutual compatibility. The children would sit at a table with a big piece of cardboard standing up between them so they could not see one another, but they could hear one another quite well. Both children would have a set of the same pictures in front of them, but of course they could not see their partner's pictures. We had the pictures mounted on boxes so that we could hide things under them. In a typical session, we would have one child hide her or his eyes for a minute while we put candy under one of the pictures, and under the matching picture in front of the child who was watching. For instance, both children had pictures of a mother tucking her children into bed, and we might put a candy under that picture. After it was hidden, the child who had watched us, and knew where the candy was, was supposed to tell the other child all about the picture where the candy

Children who seem to be users of a restricted code begin to use an elaborated code if they are given sufficient models of what is expected.

was hidden. As soon as the other child recognized which picture it was under, she or he could lift up the box and eat the candy. When this happened, the child doing the describing got to eat the candy too. We played this as a game, and all the children got a chance to talk and listen.

We judged the tape-recorded descriptions on the basis of word count and the presence or absence of adjectives, prepositional phrases and clauses; and we devised some numerical rating scales. For instance, we had one for the degree to which the child took into consideration the fact that the other child could only hear her or him and could not see the partner (the egocentricity scale). Young children frequently do not understand that another person, seated in another part of the room, sees things from a different perspective.

For example, the child who saw us hide the candy was told to tell the other child about the picture of the mother tucking her children into bed. At the most egocentric stage the child would point at the picture. It was the right picture, of course, but the other child could not see these transactions. At slightly more advanced stages, the child pointed and said, "It's under there," or something circular such as, "It's under the box with the candy under it."

Some children gave descriptions that were very similar to ones described by Bernstein. The child says something similar to, "She's putting them in there," but because the other child cannot know from this information who *she* and *them* are or where *there* is, the communication also failed. The best descriptions were more explanatory: "The candy is under a picture of a lady who is saying good night to her children."

There was quite a range in the descriptions these four-year-old children produced. Using the task just described and a few others, we divided the children into high-competence and low-competence groups, and then trained one-half of each group. The children who were producing langauge that sounded similar to adult language seemed to come from middle-income families, but the poor communicators came from both middle- and lower-income backgrounds.

We trained the children once per week for four weeks, and for only about 15 minutes per session, so that each child received about one hour of training. The training was more of the same communication game, except that each child played with me, instead of with another child. I made every effort to provide a good model for the child when it was my turn, to ask questions when it was the child's turn, and generally to steer the child toward the kind of language we wanted.

In the first week of training, we used real objects on our boxes. When it was my turn, I said, "The candy is under the box that has the mitten on it." The children soon began to make statements that were similar to mine. After this first session, no child pointed at the box and grunted when it was her or his turn. A couple of the children were not at a point in their language where they could make sentences with dependent clauses. These children made compound words instead of dependent clauses. Two of them said, "The candy under the mitten box." In the second week of training we used simple colored pictures, and in the third and fourth weeks we used more complex pictures and gave increasingly lengthy and complex descriptions. From week to week the children were giving more detailed descriptions.

After the four weeks of training, all of the children—the ones we had trained and the ones we had not trained—played the same game they had played in the original assessment. We also gave them some pictures to describe that they had never seen before. To determine whether or not increased skill in picture describing would be generalized to a related but different task, we used a Viewmaster with Christmas scenes for them to describe. Unfortunately, we did not count on the fact that the sight of a multidimensional Santa Claus might be too much for some four-year-olds. One verbal girl could do nothing but exclaim, "Santa Claus! I see Santa Claus!" We decided not to use the Viewmaster, and to base our final assessment on the descriptions of the pictures that had been used on the pretest, and on some pictures that were new to all of the children.

Our two most important scales were for the overall linguistic and semantic adequacy of the description, where a score of 1-7 could be obtained, and the scale of the egocentricity of the message which was scored from 1-6. The most adequate, least egocentric description would receive a score of 7 for adequacy and 6 for egocentricity.

On the egocentricity scale, all of the children tended to improve. Because the pretest had been conducted as a training session, this is not surprising. We also gave the post-test to two children in the school who had not been included in the pretest. These two children performed at a lower level than any child in the sample on the post-test. The children who had been trained tended to be less egocentric than the control group and to give better messages. Five out of the seven children in the training group gave descriptions that were of the least egocentric type. Only two of the eight control children gave this type of response.

On the adequacy scale, all but one of the children in the training group scored higher in the post-test than in the pretest, whereas three children in the control group did not improve.

The generalization task called upon the children to describe a picture they had never seen before. Here again, the children who had been trained provided descriptions very much like the ones they had heard from me during the training sessions. All but one of the trained children were in the highest, least egocentric category in their ratings. Only one control child gave a description of this type.

With groups this small, it is difficult to determine the extent of the changes that have taken place. Another indication of growth can be found by examining individual children's responses. For instance, one child in the training group in the pretest said, "People are sitting next to each other." Although we tried to get her to elaborate on this description, this was all she would say. Five weeks later, when called upon to describe that same picture in the post-test, she said, "The candy is under the picture with a cat, and a mother who's holding the cat, and telling her baby to pat it, I guess." Another child in the training group in the pretest said, "I don't know what it's about [prompting from examiner] I see a different . . . [prompting] I don't know . . . cat . . . [prompting] and people sleeping . . . [prompting] I don't know; that's all I can say." On the post-test, she described the same picture as follows: "The candy is under the picture of two kids sleeping on a bed, and a cat and a mother next to them, and it's a girl and a boy."

These nursery school children were eager to play our communication games and really seemed to enjoy them. As our results have shown, they proved sensitive to the models we provided, altered their basic style, and improved their ability to communicate. Children who began by grunting and pointing ended by producing good verbal descriptions. Compared with the control children, children who were trained gave more informative, more formally organized, less egocentric descriptions when they were reassessed.

There clearly are differences in young children's ability to do verbal tasks such as describing pictures so that other people can identify them. This ability may to some extent correlate with a child's background, but whether it does or not, there is no evidence that once a child uses a particular type of description she or he always uses it. Children who seem to be users of a restricted code begin to use an elaborated code if they are given sufficient models of what is expected. The training sessions facilitated the children's use of a more elaborate style. The fact that they were able to learn our style so easily indicates that elaborated code can be acquired by young children, regardless of their background.

References

Bernstein, B. "A Critique of the Concept 'Compensatory Education.'" In *Functions of Language in the Classroom,* eds. C. B. Cazden, D. Hymes, and V. P. John. New York: Teachers College Press, 1972.

Ilse Mattick

6.
The Teacher's Role in Helping Young Children Develop Language Competence

Supposing teachers provided human communication instead of "language treatment"?

My interest in the language development of young inner-city children has two sources: my own intensive study of and work with poor urban children and my numerous observations in classrooms.

There is much controversy and much confusion in the field today about programs fostering cognitive processes (and thus communications skills), about the whole child, about directive strategies, structured-cognitive or permissive-enrichment strategies, to use Bissell's (1973) terminology. We know by now which of those teach Stanford-Binet's better than the others, i.e., which one has more easily identifiable quick results in terms of specific tests.

I have real difficulties with these trends and concerns because I cannot imagine a separation between the cognitive domain and that of interaction between people. I cannot imagine such a separation for my own life; so how could I possibly for children? My ideas on the teacher's role in helping children develop language competency represent a developmental-interaction approach.

I assume that there is an interdependence between cognitive and affective development, and that the growth of intellectual functioning, such as the acquisition and organization of information, the ability to solve problems and to engage in symbolic representation cannot be divorced from

This chapter is a slightly modified version of a talk at the NAEYC national conference in 1970, first published in *Young Children* 27, no. 3 (February 1972): 133-142.

If we wish to help children become more competent communicators on a variety of subjects, in a variety of contexts, it will not do to passively wait for things to happen, and it will not do to drill.

interpersonal and intrapersonal growth processes. From this it follows that the ability to *relate* to others goes hand in hand with *talking* to others and that the development of self-esteem, self-assertion, self-confidence, and self-control are inextricably intertwined with growth in cognitive functioning and thus with competency in communication.

We should question both the celebration of the higher test scores produced by some preschool programs designated as cognitively oriented, and the educative value of the teaching procedures these programs are preparing the children to handle. A high score on instruments predicting success in an authoritarian, asocial context that denies human variety and invalidates differential needs and responses is a poor indicator of a child's ability to learn about, cope with, and have an impact on the environment. Surely, you can teach most four-year-olds to answer in long sentences, even to read—with or without the use of cleverly constructed machines or precooked teaching sequences. But does *this* assure a reading, comprehending, thinking, questioning, communicating person, capable of socially meaningful action?

It is of course not to a concern with intellectual growth that I object, but to a stated intent of widening the children's cognitive field when instead children are closed off from the exploratory learning processes; and skill acquisition is mistaken for knowledge. But let me also state clearly that I wish neither to denigrate, dismiss, nor ignore the rich knowledge that comes to us from some innovative programs. Obviously we need to learn from each other and to continually modify our methods in the light of new findings and insights. However, in my scheme of priorities, I find references to "mean length of utterances" far less fascinating or even useful than the content and affect of in-depth human communications.

The other kinds of pronouncements that concern me are those which assert that poor kids need and profit most from controlled, directive teaching. The reasons given for this kind of teaching are that poor children have fewer inner resources, difficulties in focusing, low frustration tolerance, and are not accustomed to making choices. Quite aside from the stereotyping and patronizing aspects of such statements, the consequent reasoning seems to me like saying, "Let's brick up their windows, it's dark in their apartment anyhow."

Now, I am *not* saying that didactic teaching has no place in the classroom. It does—in any classroom. A quite controlled program in which children are introduced to a rich variety of offerings will have a better chance to do something for them than one which promotes chaos and is without plans for any learning whatever. It should be clear to educators by now that neither the teacher nor the children can call all the shots if the operation is to be fruitful. There must be a balance, with deliberate action taken by teachers for specific purposes, in the context of their understanding of the children.

If we wish to help children become more competent communicators on a variety of subjects, in a variety of contexts, it will not do to just sit back and wait for things to happen and it will not do to drill. The process is much more subtle, but also much more pleasant and human. It is not even particularly difficult, given a bit of good will, some imagination, and the teacher's ability to overcome some unfortunate habits.

Important facts

For teachers there are a few important facts to keep in mind to help insure meaningful communication and then there are some specific things each teacher needs to watch for. First the facts:

1. Even the most quiet child, the one who communicates chiefly with pleading looks or eager nods or scowls is capable of using language, certainly of understanding it. I have yet to discover a nonverbal child, unless there has been a definite physical handicap; and, as we know, such handicaps occur across all social classes.

2. By the time children enter school, they already have some language; it is not something you find yourself teaching from scratch, even to a two- or three-year-old.

3. The teacher can be expected to have a considerable impact on language development. Language competency does not emerge full-bloom all of itself in an atmosphere that is a verbal or affective vacuum; it requires the experience of back and forth communication, and this calls for conscious action on the part of the teacher.

4. Language development does not mean only language production; it also means language comprehension. To a certain extent language comprehension precedes language production. However, language production is not a clear indication of language comprehension. To assume that children understand everything they say can be misleading. They may talk as they heard others talk and not necessarily understand the meaning of the words. I recall a four-year-old, for example, who walked about the classroom smiling at people and saying "Do me a favor." When the teacher said she would be glad to, the child looked utterly bewildered and just repeated the phrase. The teacher explored further to find out just what the child had in mind and discovered that the little girl did not have the slightest understanding of the term but simply liked the friendly response it evoked from people. Children easily pick up affectively important phrases without necessarily understanding them at all. (Cursing frequently goes under this heading.) Also, children like to please, and poor children in particular learn very early that adults are apt to be nicer if you agree with them. So, just because children nod their heads when you speak to them does not mean that they understand what you have said. Unless they can deal functionally with whatever they are told, we cannot be sure they understood.

For instance, I observed a three-year-old girl standing in front of the sink and saying over and over to herself, "Turn the handle of the faucet, make the water run," making no move to do so herself but looking pleadingly at the teacher to produce some water. Even when children deal functionally with the teacher's pronouncements it could mean they understood the words, but it could also mean that they understood only the context.

Another example is Janice, almost five, who was sitting at the table stringing beads. One of the beads rolled off the table. She wondered where it was and I told her that it was "under the table." Since she immediately dived under the table and recovered her bead I assumed that she understood what I had said. However, it later occurred to me that as I said "under the table" I looked under the table and pointed with my finger. So I made a little experiment. Every day when Janice came to school she was in the habit of making a drawing with chalk on the easel chalkboard. There was a box of chalk on the easel tray. Before Janice came in the next time, I took the tray and put it on the windowsill right next to the easel. Needless to say, Janice noticed that her chalk was not in its proper place and set up a howl. I said that the chalk was right behind her on the windowsill, restraining myself from either pointing to or looking at that place. Janice looked me straight in the eye, smiled and said, "Yes, but where is it?" I found out subsequently that she was just as unable to find something "under the table" when I did not give other than language cues (for more details see Mattick 1965, 1967).

5. Children will use language more fully if there is something of importance to them to communicate, that is, of importance to *them,* not to the teacher. This is a crucial issue and one most frequently ignored by teachers, investigators, and program planners. I observed a teacher trying his very best to get children interested in a story he was reading to them. It was a perfectly lovely story and it was reasonable for him to assume that it would catch the children's interest. However, the children's responses were meager; a fine example of the monosyllabic language production researchers are fond of quoting as typical of poor children. Then the teacher, who did not seem to give in to frustration and become irritable but who remained sensitively aware of his children's reactions, discovered that a number of them were straining to listen to something outdoors. The teacher switched from the topic of his story to the topic of the noise outside. Immediately the children launched into a linguistically complex discussion about the garbage truck they heard outside. The difference between the levels of the responses to the two topics was striking. Clearly, back and forth verbal interactions are more likely to be prolonged if initiated by the child, in contrast to those that are thrust upon the child to extract teacher-specified content.

6. It is much harder for a teacher to interact verbally with children whose responses she either does not understand or who do not give clear signs of what part of her message they have understood. Often in classrooms where there is a socioeconomic mix of children, verbal interactions tend to be most prolonged and varied between the teacher and the children who are most tuned in to conversing with adults, i.e., those who need it the least. It is, however, inexcusable for teachers to "cop-out," as it is their responsibility to initiate interaction among children and to bring children

to the point where they themselves can interact spontaneously.

7. While the quality of the interaction is far more important than the quantity, still, *prolonged* back and forth interaction contributes to the growth of language complexity, particularly if it is varied and rich. And this takes us back to the fifth point concerning communication which is of importance.

This is just an introduction to the discussion of language development in relation to a preschool program. I have not even mentioned the factual knowledge available concerning dialects and other specific linguistic dimensions related to social life styles, such information can be found elsewhere (e.g., Bernstein 1973, Cazden 1972, Dale 1976, Labov 1972, and Williams 1970). We are still just beginning to be aware of their precise implications for communication attainments and/or mismatches; and it is certain that teachers must become sensitive to and knowledgeable about these facts as well. But the above seven points hopefully may serve as a guide for dispelling some of the bewilderment that teachers may have experienced in the face of the barrage of prescriptive notions about "language treatment" in recent years.

Questions to ask yourself

What about the teacher's tasks, referred to as "teaching strategies," or "interaction-skills," or whatever term is "in" for you? If language is to be used as a means of finding solutions to problems, of showing interest and concern, of eliciting thinking responses, of presenting information of interest to the children, of guiding children into elaborated activities and more complex cognitive organization, and as a means of helping them control their own behavior, then I would suggest that as a teacher you ask yourself the following questions when interacting verbally with children.

● Is this a back and forth interaction, or a monologue on my part? Do I encourage the children to engage me in conversation; i.e., is the topic of relevance to the child and does it therefore give better chances for rich and complex language expression? Who does most of the talking, the child or me?

● Are my questions open- or close-ended: i.e., are they thought-inducing ("What do you suppose the boy did with the bird?") or are they correct-answer questions ("What did the boy find?")? The former encourages *thinking responses* and these lead to much more complex communicative skills and to much better chances for fluent conversation than the latter, which are apt to produce one-word responses ("bird"), or bewildered looks as if the child has forgotten or is not sure what answers the teacher wants, or perhaps even contemptuous looks if it occurs to the child, as it often does to kids, that the answer is self-evident and therefore the question is silly.

It can be assumed that children offer answers to close-ended questions to satisfy the teacher. This does not mobilize their communicative abilities.

Prolonged back-and-forth interaction contributes to the growth of language complexity, particularly if it is varied and rich.

Thought-provoking questions, on the other hand, lead to greater clarity in thinking and expression; at least they open up this possibility. At the very least they signal to children that the teacher respects their thoughts, rather than that they are put on trial. It is not really difficult to show this respect (providing the teacher feels genuine respect for children) and to promote thinking responses.

In a classroom I watched two children fighting. Each of the two boys was pushing a small car along the floor; they were practically tripping each other to get ahead of one another and both of them were screaming at the top of their lungs, "cheating, cheating." To the teacher's calm query, "What seems to be the trouble?" both shouted, "He's cheating." The teacher asked, "In which way?" with real interest in her voice. One boy went into a long complicated explanation of the race they were having and the other boy expressed in a complex sentence his frustration that he could not get ahead of the first boy. The teacher commented that in races people usually had a starting line. This triggered a discussion between the boys about where and how they might make a starting line as well as a finish line. A little later in the same classroom a girl asserted to the teacher that another girl's drawing was "no good." Again the teacher asked, with real interest, "How do you mean?"; thus encouraging the girl to be more specific about her reaction to the drawing. On each of these two occasions the teacher elicited verbalizations borne of further thinking.

As a teacher I would watch for the *specificity* of my responses. If we want to move children from a global, nonspecific mode such as the familiar "lookit teach" or "gimme dis" to focused communication, it is incumbent upon us to provide a model of highly specific verbalizations. Here are two examples that illustrate the difference, although both focus on the same indispensable gadget.

In one day care center a five-year-old boy ran out of the classroom with a stapler in his hand. In the hallway he encountered the director. The boy smiled, thrust the stapler out at the director and said, "Here, take it." The director smiled and said, "Oh, you're done with this." The child nodded and returned to his room. Contrast this episode with the following excerpt from a tape recorded observation in another center. The teacher said (to a five-year-old), "Oh, Ronny, do me a favor. I borrowed this stapler from Miss Brown's desk to fix the book Larry made, so that we could see the words. You give this stapler back to Miss Brown, please, and tell her she was not there when we borrowed it; and that she did not know that we borrowed it. Tell her thank you for the stapler, okay?" Naturally I was curious to observe what would happen and so I followed the child to the director's office. Ronny not only conveyed the message in long complex sentences, but he used different expressions rather than recalling the teacher's words verbatim. I cite this example in detail because it shows that specificity does *not* imply feeding a child pap, i.e., simplifying language to meaningless artificial structures that a child would neither use nor normally encounter in the real world (as in "Jump, Spot, jump. See Spot jump."). It does mean, however, that factual information embedded in a meaningful interaction context needs to replace nonspecific interchanges about "it" or "this."

• Also, one might ask oneself: "Am I moralizing, i.e., am I telling children how they should be thinking and feeling instead of accepting the way they do, or say they do?" It is hard for teachers to resist preaching and moralizing—it is one of the guaranteed ways to turn off back and forth verbal interactions and to render children unsure of themselves and of their own opinions. It also invites defiant responses.

• Do I really listen to children? Or do I interrupt with an answer as soon as I think I have guessed what a child means, or even with an answer that fits my own preconceptions or needs for control? Research findings have confirmed what children have known for a long time: namely, that teachers tend to pay scant attention to their, the children's, efforts at communicating. Sometimes not even the verbalizations themselves are heeded. More often there is a facile response to the words, but not to the message the child is trying to convey. The teacher then has "listened"; but her response is in terms of her own rather than the child's intent. While the resultant communication mismatch is prevalent between middle-class teachers and children of working-class parents, it is by no means restricted to this group.

The following is one example of many that demonstrates nonlistening to a highly pertinent communication: The teacher walked to the easel where a five-year-old had been painting for some minutes with energy, concentration, and wild abandon. The paper was dripping with bright reds and yellows, as were the boy's hands and arms. He had just stepped back and surveyed his picture with a frown. With the teacher next to him he again reached for a brush, made a wide sweeping stroke over the paper and the easel frame and said softly: "Bye-bye, bus." With a disdainful look at the dripping paint the teacher retorted: "Bye-bye, painting, Georgie, go wash your hands." The teacher here "listened" to the boy's words; they gave her an opening to terminate his messy activity in an overtly friendly manner. She missed completely, however, his intended communication (easily solicited by this observer) about his mother going far away on a bus.

It is even more common for teachers to cut off genuine curiosity and a spirit of inquiry by not listening: I observed a group of children working with mirror cards; one girl was holding the mirror toward the window and as it caught the reflection of the sun she called excitedly, "Lookit, it's burning!" The other children looked up and one girl asked: "Why it burn, teach?" The teacher's verbatim response was: "What's my name, Louise? My name is Miss Jenks, not 'teach'; if Nancy would be using the mirror the right way it would not burn." This type of inappropriate and inaccurate as well as chilling response is all too common, particularly in programs dedicated to furthering cognitive skills.

There is little reason for children to make the effort to solicit information, to state their intentions, their quests, or vague notions in a distinct manner or, for that matter, to speak much at all if nobody *listens*. It is only on the basis of really listening that the teacher can (a) request more details; (b) help children identify the issues, ideas, feelings, and give them names; and (c) project various alternatives for the children to consider; in other words, create the possibility for a sequence in language proficiency and expressiveness.

• Is my language production geared to the children's understanding and at the same time expanding the child's existing language, giving them new words for more complex operations? Many teachers talk down to children while at the same time communicating thought-associations that cannot possibly make sense to children. For example, I recently heard a child complain to the teacher, "I got no scissors." The teacher's response in a "cute" voice was "Oh, I wish our scissors would hurry up and come." I wonder if the child shared my vision of scissors marching up the stairs into the room? Of course, while indulging in this fantasy, resulting from taking the teacher's actual words at face value—as kids usually do—I also understood that the teacher had ordered new scissors and was awaiting their arrival. It is not reasonable to expect a young child to make this assumption.

• Do I finish my sentences or do I leave the children hanging in midair?

Recently, I heard a teacher say to her class: "Put your name on your picture because when it's time to go home. . . ." On another visit, the teacher said to the children, "Let's see what I can do for you." She said this on seven different occasions during one morning without ever following through with one more word or action.

• Do I avoid using pat phrases over and over again? There is a kind of stereotyped early childhood education lingo that is deadly for developing communicative competency in children. For example, using the phrase, "What's the matter?" each time something goes wrong as opposed to varying it with, "What is happening over here?" or "How are you getting along?" Do children hear, "It's time now to wash hands, it's time now for music," etc., every day, or are a variety of expressions used that are designed to help children think about solutions or about some concept?

• Do I involve children in activities that lend themselves easily to promoting—and might even necessitate—verbal interactions? Just to name a few: word games, cooking (involving verbal choices and instructions), puppets, grocery store, dramatic play, etc., aside from the obvious ones of storytelling, "making my own book" projects, putting captions to pictures, describing a trip or other special occasion, and writing to a friend.

• Is there a maximum chance for children to converse with each other? It is amazing how frequently children are prevented from talking to each other. The most prevalent teacher vocabulary item that I hear in classrooms is "Sh-sh." For some reason it seems to make teachers nervous to have children converse freely with each other. I believe this is mainly due to the extraordinary reluctance shared by many adults, but especially by a great many teachers, to refrain from exerting arbitrary control over children. There is also, of course, the completely erroneous but persistent assumption that children learn better when they are quiet. Such assumptions, although long disproved, die slowly because we tend to replicate that which happened to us, just as the children will be apt to replicate that which they experience. To say that children need the freedom to converse is not to say that we should promote bedlam or chaos. On the contrary, the kind of organization where rich interactions can take place is of real importance. A staggering number of opportunities are lost for engaging children in meaningful verbal interaction if there are no predictable and accepted ground rules for conduct and/or if the children find themselves in a generally unpredictable environment. In other words, unless teachers encourage the development of an organization of classroom life that reflects their well-thought-out conceptions about education, their efforts are likely to fail. But let us return to the specific teaching strategies that promote and enhance language development.

• Do I take action to involve children in verbal communications when there is the opportunity? While talk among children is apt to develop naturally in familiar surroundings, in the school setting the teacher may need to do far more than just wait for children to talk to her or him or even to each other in a group. Certain children are used to initiating and maintaining verbal interactions at an early age. For others, this process may need active encouragement by an adult who is open and sensitive to alternative styles of communications, both verbal and nonverbal. Appropriate support that facilitates ever more complex symbolic representation, in play activities and in language, may be sadly lacking, as seen in the following example. A teacher asked a boy, almost five years old, to tell her about his block building. He looked up, smiled, pointed to the last block he put on top of the structure and said, "De block on top." The teacher nodded and walked off, accepting his limited "concrete" answer without making any attempt to help this boy verbalize other relevant information about his activity and thus be aided in organizing his experience for himself.

Do I involve children in activities that lend themselves easily to promoting—and might even necessitate— verbal interactions?

• Consider the following: is verbal interaction related to the real world and more importantly to the child's real world? The distinction to be made here is between a teacher engaging a child in verbalization (perhaps of measurements related to water play or cooking), as it fits meaningfully into the child's activity, and a teacher who artificially imposes learning tasks quite remote from the children's priorities, in the contexts she selects. An example for the latter is this scene, observed in a kindergarten: The children were eager to have their milk and crackers. The teacher poured their milk for them. I wondered why these five-year-old capable children were not allowed to pour their own milk; but I quickly noticed that the teacher poured differential amounts of milk into several of the glasses. She then proceeded to launch into a "language and math lesson" on the amounts of milk in different glasses. "Billy's glass is three-fourths full, Jimmy's glass is one-half full, Sarah's glass is one-half empty, Jane's glass is one-fourth full." Her lesson was certainly related to the real world but was it the children's real world at this time? They clearly were concentrating on getting their snacks as well as reacting to the teacher giving some children less milk than to others. I have never seen as much milk gulped, spilled, and noisily slurped, nor as many ears closed.

Drilling children in linguistic forms can turn the kids off in a hurry, just as quickly as asking them to produce correct answers to questions. You can teach a child to use the correct words in the right places, such as *under, over, around, into, or.* But if you want more than a mechanical repertoire of words, if you want understanding and transferability, be sure the words are attached to action or demonstrations of what the words actually mean in the context of the child's experiential field and are not imbedded in abstractions.

It is no accident that a word like *or* is usually missing from the vocabulary of children who have had few options. How often during the course of the day do we as teachers give children legitimate choices? (I stress "legitimate" because a child dripping with fingerpaint is not being given a choice if asked, "Do you want to wash your hands now?") How often do you give a child a piece of construction paper, of whatever color happens to come into your hands; and how often do you ask him which color he prefers? Opportunities for legitimate decision-making by children, affecting their own increasing ability to act upon the real world, constitute significant learning experiences of value far beyond the gains in linguistic maturation.

• There is one last question that teachers need to ask themselves and it is the most important one when communicating with young children: Does the interaction take place in the context of mutual trust and respect; a mutual trust and respect based on the teacher's genuine friendliness, unconditional acceptance, warmth, empathy, interest? It is *this* that makes language flow, that makes it worthwhile and exciting for the children to talk freely and motivates them to acquire communication competency.

References

Bernstein, B. *Class, Codes and Control.* St. Albans, England: Paladin, 1973. (Chapter 9 "Social Class, Language and Socialization" pp. 193-213.)
Bissell, J. S. "The Cognitive Effects of Pre-School Programs for Disadvantaged Children." In *Revisiting Early Childhood Education,* ed. J. L. Frost. New York: Holt, Rinehart & Winston, 1973. (pp. 223-240)

Cazden, C. B. *Child Language and Education.* New York: Holt, Rinehart & Winston, 1972. (particularly Chapters 6 and 7)

Cazden, C. B.; John, V. P.; and Hymes, D., eds. *Function of Language in the Classroom.* New York: Teachers College Press, Columbia University, 1972.

Dale, P. S. *Language Development.* 2nd ed. New York: Holt, Rinehart & Winston, 1976. (Chapter 10 "Dialect Differences and Language Development," pp. 268-294)

Labov, W. *Language in the Inner-City.* Philadelphia: University of Pennsylvania Press, 1972.

Mattick, I. "Adaptations of Nursery School Techniques to Deprived Children." *Journal of the American Academy of Child Psychiatry* 4 no. 4 (Oct. 1965): 670-700.

Mattick, I. "Description of the Children." In *The Drifters,* ed. E. Pavenstedt. Boston: Little, Brown, 1967. (see section on language and cognitive development, pp. 71-80)

Williams, F., ed. *Language and Poverty.* Chicago: Markham, 1970.

Courtney B. Cazden
Betty H. Bryant
and Melissa A. Tillman

7.
Making It and Going Home: The Attitudes of Black People Toward Language Education

In a report on school demonstrations in the South, *New York Times* reporter Roy Reed said:

> There is no evidence of any central stimulus or control in this year's expanded protests. All have been initiated locally, often by [Blacks] unaccustomed to leadership. However, a common theme runs through all of them. A growing number of Southern Blacks, like their Northern brothers, are reported to be impatient at having public decisions affecting their lives made by white men without consulting the Black community.

We believe the Black community should be consulted, about questions of educational objectives as well as school organization. In the preschool field, one of the most important objectives is some kind of language education. How do people in the Black community feel about standard English and Black dialect? What kind of preschool language education do they want for their children?

We asked these two questions of five groups of people in Roxbury, the Black community in Boston: parents of children in two preschools, teachers and teacher aides in the same schools and a group of community leaders invited to come together for this discussion. Melissa Tillman conducted the discussions. All participants in all of the groups were Black.

Reprinted with permission and additions from the *Harvard Graduate School of Education Association Bulletin* 14, no. 3 (Spring 1970): 4-9.

Parents

Discussions were held with parents of children in two preschools. The schools were picked to provide a possible contrast in degree of influence of Black Power ideology. One school is physically close to the center of Black Power activity in Roxbury, and has been more influenced by it through its personnel and educational program. For example, Black artists and musicians have come to share their skills with the children and help build their self-conscious pride in being Black. The other school is both physically farther away and less changed in personnel and program over the past few years. In the end, difficulties with the tape recorder made it impossible to record the discussion among the six parents at the more "traditional" school, and so all excerpts below are from the five parents in the first group. Melissa Tillman, who picked the groups and conducted the discussions, heard no evidence of contrasting opinions between the two groups.

Parent: My first language, as I learned it, was slave language, 'cause it was not by choice.

Parent: What we gonna stop is "not by choice." We want proper English taught.

Parent: Right! Get rid of it. Throw it away. Tell the kids, "Hey, don't speak that junk. Forget it."

Parent: I really don't feel it's junk, because, sometimes, trying to express themselves, especially around the house, to show that this three-, four-, or five-year-old is grown up and fits in with his family, he will use slang expression.

Parent: Why is street English, or whatever it is, why is that important at all? Or why should it be important? Like the way my mother speak—she's always spoken all broken up, and she's never cared one way or the other—for the same reason that she's never voted. So what? But why is it important to speak, uh, wrong—uh, not wrong—it's a different language. Why is it important to speak a slave language?

Parent: Well, I think most of us have two faces anyway. I think we speak one way at home and to our children and another way when we're in the street and when we're associating with other people. But I think that as long as you get the message—some people can put the message across most emphatically in their language.

Parent: Slang has more power than proper language.

Parent: But that isn't really slang. That's like—you know—that's another language.

Parent: I have tried to teach my children proper English.

Interviewer: Why?

Parent: I always thought it sounded cuter for a child to be able to speak correctly at a young age than it did for them to use, you know, their little mannerisms that they get naturally. I have quite a few children. I have seven. So with some of the children it worked. And some of my children now still talk as if they were hit on the end of their tongue with a hammer—that's the only way I can describe it. And I know I have corrected them over and over. It's just a speech habit, a pattern that they've gotten into. But as far as correct usage, most of my children know the correction even if they don't say the proper thing. They know. But I don't feel ashamed if they don't say the right thing, you know.

Interviewer: Some educators feel that if school work was presented in the child's language—Black English—it would be easier for the child to grasp the concepts. What are your feelings about this?

Parent: In the preschool, I think it should be standard English.

Interviewer: Why?

Parent: Well, if you teach your child standard English in school, the child is gonna learn Black English or street language out of school anyway. It's as if a child's home language is Spanish or German and they go to an English school so that they learn English. Right? In most cases, they will learn the English and, in addition, they will speak the, more or less, home language because they're gonna hear more home language than school language, or about as much.

Parent: I think it's sorta hard to really change a child's pattern of thinking, because even though you tell them a thousand times, you sometimes result in confusing them. So I think that in some cases, their home language or their language patterns for their age—if it fits what they're saying—should stand as is.

Parent: I think they should learn while they're young because the longer they wait, the harder it's going to be for them to—

Parent: (interrupts)—build a good foundation—right from the start.

Parent: Well, if my son said, "Look at him hat," then I would say, "Yes, I see *his* hat."

Parent: Right, right. You have in turn given him proper English.

Parent: You have to bring it to his attention. Then I wouldn't push the issue. But I would give him the correct words.

Interviewer: What do you expect your preschool teachers to do when they're recording your child's language in experience charts? If a child said, "him's hat," would you want the teacher to write that or write down, "his hat?"

Parent: Well, if it was my child, I'd want you to correct him.

Parent: If you went to a job, and one was talking standard English and one was talking slang, they're not going to go by what you know and what you can do. They're going to go by how you're talking, how you present yourself.

Parent: Today, my husband is afraid to open his mouth in public.

Parent: Why?

Parent: Because he knows the minute he opens his mouth, it comes out wrong. He says things like "more better."

Parent: The child should be taught standard English in the school now.

Parent: Right now. As soon as a child starts talking, in his home, at his table, his parents should speak proper English!

Parent: Well, what about the teacher? They should speak too. That's what they're there for. They're there to teach the child correctly—anything— math, history, English.

Parent: O.K. I just want to make sure you and I are thinking together.

Parent: We all think the same thing. That was right from the "git go."

Whether these Black parents reject Black English because it originated in the slave experience or appreciate it for its power of expression, they feel it has no place in school. They realize that "Most of us have two faces." But since children will learn to speak Black English at home anyway, the job of the school is to teach in, and teach, standard English.

Where feelings among Black parents are this deep and this negative, any program which attempts to teach in a nonstandard dialect is likely to encounter strong opposition. This does not mean that an attempt should not be made if there were clear evidence (which doesn't yet exist) that it would increase the likelihood of success with goals the parents do want, such as literacy in standard English. But it does mean that full discussion with the parents would be essential.

Teachers

Discussions were held with teachers and teacher aides from the same two preschools. Originally we planned to talk with teachers and aides separately, since the aides represent a distinct group in social class background and present social mobility. But the resulting groups were so small that the staff groups were combined.

Teacher: There are certain common words that are the same all over amongst Black people, which might be one reason for encouraging Black language—to build that sense of unity.

Teacher: Black people and their way of talking is sort of—it has a rhythm to it. And I think this is one of the things that sort of makes it unique.

Teacher: I think Black language relates. You know, it really gets to the point.

Teacher: But, Black people, they also change. I mean, you'll find Black people talking white and you'll find Black people talking Black. You know, doing what you call "going home."

Teacher: Well, you can't weed it out [eliminate dialect].

Teacher: Besides, it won't be weeded out. In fact, more is going to be added to it.

Teacher: One thing you have to bear in mind—their Black language is part of their Blackness. And until, if ever, the whole Black society changes their way of speech, it'll be taking something from them.

Teacher: I think with us here, we realize that a child's life goals may change, and he may move out of this particular community. And I think the big question is whether or not he could survive with his language in a white community or in the white society. Some people think he needs standard English, white English, and has to talk that way. But I know lots of people who are thinking about whether or not he *has* to talk that way. *Does he?* I think just as an example, T.V. and everything else is all of a sudden flooded with people who do not speak standard English on a lot of the programs. And yet people are certainly getting their message across either by very, very strong, powerful voices and strong wills, or else a personality appeal, maybe. So it's almost like the question is, have we been living under this big illusion along with all the other illusions? Is language just another one—that we can't make it in this world? The thing is now, whether or not it's really worthwhile to worry about whether a child speaks in a certain way.

Teacher: I feel that the children later on in life are going out into business programs and they're going to go to school to be taught English. And, I think that they should be taught to use it properly.

Teacher: I think this was my feeling about language. They're gonna go to school. They're gonna be taught standard English and I think it should be presented to them, [but] they're gonna need their own, in their own community.

Teacher: It seems to me that we've gotta do an awful lot of things because of the times and the age that we're living in. We've got to give them the two ways. But, then again, at the same time, I think—I guess I feel sort of torn—that we oughta not be worrying so much about whether somebody's English sounds correctly standard and really appreciate a little bit more what we do have, what the kids do bring.

Teacher: I think the language concepts, the thinking skills are really what you want to give a child. You'd like to see him to be able to think more creatively than maybe other people and the situations around him to allow him to be.

Interviewer: Does teaching standard English alter the child's view of his family or community?

Teacher: I think it all depends upon how it's presented to him. If it's presented to him in a way where it's knocking what he's been used to hearing, of course he'll have second thoughts about it, his family, his friends, and where he's come from and where he's going. That type of problem. But, I think standard English can be presented to him in such a way that he has no feelings. It's just that he's learned another way to speak.

Teacher: But, I don't think it happens that way very often. It usually happens that this is the better way—that, you know, he's given either bad or good. Can you really teach standard English and not negate the dialect? Can you really do this where standard English is sort of thrust from so many sides, all through school, from a white oriented society? Now it would be interesting to compare the child who went completely to Black schools, or to community schools. Realistically that hasn't happened, hasn't been happening—that a child doesn't begin to feel that his language is a little bit inferior, somewhere along the way.

Teacher: Being here, we have to be aware of where we're at. That has a lot to do with language. Survival—in this area, survival is the main thing. If you're going to be weak and you can't stand up, lots of times it's your mouth that will help you stand up. Other times it's physical, but still lots of times your mouth will help you.

These teachers express more conflict about language than the parents did. Survival is the main thing, and "lots of times your mouth can help you." Within the Black community, survival requires street language. Maybe it's an illusion—a myth with no basis in fact—that survival in relationship with the white community requires standard English. And maybe we should be paying more attention to language for thinking and for creativity.

Community Leaders

Five community leaders assembled by invitation for an evening meeting at Melissa Tillman's apartment in Roxbury. The group did not include more conservative church leaders at one end nor any member of the Black Panthers at the other end, though we tried to include them. It did include some of the more vocal, articulate and militant leadership. And we believe it reflects the opinions of the larger group of community leaders who are most likely to speak out on educational questions whenever there is an opportunity to do so.

Community Leader: I would say definitely that there is a Black language, and it reflects the—let's see—the resistance, a culture of resistance—of passive resistance. You know, in terms of level communicating—talking under your breath. There are all different kinds of ways, of gestures, that are reflections of a passive resistance. (group agreement)
Community Leader: Beautiful!
Community Leader: (continues)—That's number one. The other important thing in the Black language has to do with predominantly low income existence which has a limit. There's a limit of resources in that community. In other words, that's why Black language may not equal middle class language or American language in terms of the number of different symbols, the number of different words for things.
Community Leader: Both are reactive or reactionary kinds of situations to the dominant group. So, therefore, we aren't talking about language, Black language, *per se,* such as Chinese or some Indian dialect or some Russian dialect, which is a separate entity. You see what I mean?
Community Leader: Yeah, but I disagree. Regardless of the means by which we got to what we have, we've got it.
Community Leader: But it makes a difference when you look at it from a standpoint of a parent who says, "I want my child to do better than I." Then, you have to talk about the child being more adaptive.

How do people in the Black community feel about standard English and Black dialect? What kind of pre-school language education do they want for their children?

Community Leader: I don't believe that, in the first place. I don't believe that the way the kids talk is a result of hearing their parents—passively resist. Now you show me how!

Community Leader: I'm not gonna deal with that from the standpoint of a conscious perception of the child's response to the adult as a social being. It happens because it's transmitted by the parent at a feeling level where the first educational process takes place.

Interviewer: If, as you say, the language is a part of the culture, that grew up for very specific reasons, do you think these language programs are going to be able to change that?

Community Leader: Not unless the culture changes.

Community Leader: The relationship that Black people hold to white people, I don't think it's radically gonna change. I think Black language— it's my freedom from white people. When there's several white people in the room and there's something that I want to know about—

Community Leader: (interrupts)—you use your own language.

Community Leader: I immediately go into this Black thing.

Community Leader: They [children] ought to have both of them, too.

Interviewer: What kind of language program do you want for your children?

Community Leader: If we're going to talk about education as it now stands, then it means—they need to learn to talk in standard English if they're gonna do well in school—unless schools change. You have to decide if you think standard English is important. I do! I do!

Community Leader: We have to teach this child to function in the world under the system which exists.

Community Leader: The way of the world is—the system may be wrong, it may be right.

Community Leader: The issue is not the way the world is. The tendency is for us to do it as we see it to come or to be.

Community Leader: No! That's not the tendency—

Community Leader: (interrupts) No! No! We always tend to do what we think it will be. Now we may not articulate this or deal with it. But, that's what's happening.

Community Leader: People who have control of the language are hustlers. You know, they can really make it. You don't have to have any substance in terms of ideas—just rap a good game. In that context, language is very important. (general agreement)

Community Leader: I'll buy that!

Interviewer: What is it about the hustler's language, when he's at his best and hustling well, that's different from that school language?

Community Leader: I think, within the context of each of these settings, nothing. There's no difference. In other words, you have to examine the setting in which people have to function. And, within his setting, his [language] works for him. Within that school setting, if that school dictates a certain set of skills, that's what people gonna have to learn. As long as they're within that setting. See, my question is the people who control the setting, and what they see as important and not important.

Community Leader: But, it is important how you think of that. It's O.K. for someone to say you should be taking some other position about how you respond and how you function. But, damned if it's O.K. if I have to start from the basis that they're somehow correct. That's a bad scene. You're going to pay a price for my having to make the transition. We gotta talk about who's gonna set the tone. Who's gonna set the standard. I don't buy that because Whitey's in power I'm gonna accept his standard in order to succeed—except superficially!

Community Leader: Another thing that's very important is that Black people in many ways may have survived because they have another language. I feel, in many ways, Blacks have been able to survive through use of their own cultural reflections—through their own language. And I'm sort of afraid of people who will devise early childhood language programs to change the language of a kid. And those same people will not fight for increased income, social status, power.

Community Leader: (interrupts) I second the motion.

Community Leader: (continues) I feel that there's an inherent kind of racism involved in that. And what may be happening with those kinds of programs is a very slow and insidious means to really destroy Black people through their kids.

Community Leader: This is the point! This is the point!

Community Leader: (continues) And I think the approaches to teaching kids has got to be controlled.

Community Leader: We've been sold the bag that language education is our way out—and a part of it is speaking the way they speak—which is not necessarily true. It's generally not true, as a matter of fact. The kind of thing that would teach them control over what they do, would lead to control over their environment—I'm saying that just learning language is not going to make them do it. There's something about starting very early to control just your environment and your learning processes that moves you on to the position of feeling, whether it's true or not, that you do have some control. And language without that is—is holding out false hopes.

Community leaders, in their roles as leaders, are farther away from the direct socialization of young children than parents and teachers. Their concern is to reflect the current needs of the group in educational policy, and at the same time to institute those changes which will move the group forward. In comparison to both the parents and teachers, these leaders are more positive in their evaluation of Black English, and more openly resentful that it is always Black people who have to change. "Survival" for them means not only economic survival in a white-dominated society but also psychological survival as a people. Language for intra-group solidarity, for "going home," is as important as language for "making it." And in education, the myth that language education is the way out is not only questioned but rejected. Control over the environment is critical. Language programs without that control are at best false hopes, and at worst insidious racism.

Courtney B. Cazden
Joan C. Baratz
William Labov
Francis H. Palmer

8.
Language Development in Day Care Programs

One of the responsibilities of any day care center is to extend each child's verbal abilities. This means continuing his learning of the structure of his native language or dialect, and probably helping him learn standard English (SE) as well. It means extending his repertoire of words and meanings for talking about the objects, events and ideas in his expanding world. It means giving him rich opportunities to use language for private thought and for social communication in ways satisfying to him and important for school success.

In this chapter we will talk about the conditions that should be present if this responsibility is to be fulfilled. We will not discuss specific curriculum options because these will be presented in other documents on day care being prepared simultaneously with this one. Instead, we will concentrate on more general conditions which are important, whatever the prevailing curriculum philosophy and practice. We will concentrate on the traditional preschool years of three to five, with occasional comments on children younger and older.

Discussion is divided into three main sections: knowledge about language development; knowledge about language differences; and suggestions for operating day care centers for maximum language development.

Reprinted with permission from *Day Care: Resources for Decisions*, ed. E. H. Grotberg. Washington, D.C.: OEO Office of Planning Research and Evaluation, n.d.

Language development

By and large, children do not learn language from their teachers. Most children come to school, even to preschool, with basic knowledge of the grammar of their native language. What we know of this acquisition process has been described in Chapter 1.

While the course of language development is similar for all children, individual differences in the rate of development will be striking in any day care center. These differences appear in both speaking and understanding, and they pose special problems for teachers.

For example, at age 2½, many children are talking a great deal while others do not utter a word. The child who talks well at age two is not necessarily brighter, nor will he necessarily be more verbally capable at age three. A little later in life, roughly from 3½ on, there is a relationship between how verbal a child is and how verbal he will be in the future. But in the earliest months of talking, this is not the case.

Individual differences in amount of talking in very young children pose a specified problem for teachers because adults tend to talk more to children who talk back. (Adults like reinforcement too.) And so, unwittingly, a day care center may magnify natural differences. Talkers who are reinforced for talking by someone they like and trust will talk even more; nontalkers may be even less inclined to talk if they are ignored. Teachers must be exceedingly careful how they distribute their attention during the day.

Variability among children in understanding language is probably as great as variability in talking. Consider, for example, Palmer's (1970) research on New York City children's comprehension of words for basic concepts like *on top of, fast, wet, same as* or *many*. Children were asked to demonstrate their understanding by manipulating objects. For instance, using a tow truck and a car, children were asked to "make the car go *up*" and "make the car go *down*." Of 50 such concepts, some children at age two understood only six or seven while other children understood as many as 40.

Some concepts, and the words associated with them, are easier than others and learned earlier by most children. For example, of 240 children from three ethnic groups in Palmer's study, the following percentages of all children responded correctly to particular words:

on top of	(93%)	**slow**	(29%)
into	(82%)	**biggest**	(26%)
open	(74%)	**under**	(18%)
wet	(68%)	**around**	(10%)

The comprehension vocabulary of a child is seldom as well recognized by those about him as his productive vocabulary. Yet good teaching presumably requires that the teacher talk with each child in words he can understand while helping him always to learn more. Teachers need to listen sensitively to children in a variety of situations.

A child's background may influence his knowledge about such concepts, even as early as age two. For reasons we don't understand, the Puerto Rican children in Palmer's study were considerably better in responding to concepts of movement such as *fast* and *slow*, even though the three groups were matched for socioeconomic status. Thus while some concepts are generally more difficult for children, the immediate home environment contributes to what specific concepts children understand. The specific population that a day care program serves will influence what knowledge children bring to the program.

In a center where age groups are mixed, the extent of individual differences will of course be greater. By age three, most children have learned to comprehend many of the simpler concepts. For example, Palmer found that, in the same sample of 240 children at age three, 70 percent of the children comprehended the concept *under,* whereas only 18 percent had done so at age two. Concepts which are still very difficult for the three-year-old were *bottom, backward,* and *side.* Still other concepts, such as *same* and *different,* remain difficult for children even when they are four.

Words representing concepts like *into* are learned first in specific situations. Even when a child shows that he understands the message *Put the toy into the box,* we cannot assume that he has a general understanding of the spatial relationship *into.* He may simply know what one normally does with toys and boxes. One characteristic of language learning is growth from meanings which are situation-bound to meanings which are situation-free, and children will vary in how situation-bound their meanings of particular words are. Even with words that children may "know" in a limited sense, teachers should try to use those words in a rich variety of contexts.

Finally, a word about differences that correlate with social class. Language development in the growing child is partly a function of the education and occupation of his parents. This is particularly true for knowledge of word meanings, which is what most language tests (and also some intelligence tests) evaluate. This fact has led some teachers and researchers to infer that differences in all forms of language development begin very early in life, shortly after the child begins to talk. This is not the case.

The language comprehension of . . . [Black] boys of widely varying socioeconomic classes was compared at age 2/0, 2/8, 3/0 and 3/8. Care was taken to make sure that each child was comfortable in the testing situation so that four to 15 hours were required to finish the test battery, depending on the child's age and individual characteristics. No significant socioeconomic class differences were shown. Comprehension does vary according to socioeconomic class at about age 4½. These socioeconomic class differences emerge first at the extreme of parents with exceptional educations, and a select group at the highest end of the socioeconomic scale may perform better as early as three. But no differences between the child of average parents and the child of ghetto parents emerges until 4½ (Palmer 1970).

This fact has significant implications for preschool education, . . . [because] from two to 4½ are years in which children frequently are first placed in day care centers and nursery schools. We can reduce the differences which would otherwise emerge.

Language differences

Most children differ from their teachers in the language system (the grammar) that they use. They also differ among themselves in verbal styles. It is not possible to plan effective educational programs without taking these differences into account.

Differences in grammatical systems

One important source of language differences is, of course, the foreign language background of many children. Some children of immigrant families come to school without knowing English; however, in most cases they are already using English before the age of five. In the United States, the normal pattern has been for parents to promote the use of English by their children; knowledge of the foreign language is only passive for these children, even in the first native generation. The Italian or Yiddish backgrounds of many first generation children has surprisingly little influence upon their English.

This pattern of the decline of the immigrant language is evident among Puerto Ricans, although the continuous exchange with Puerto Rico obscures it and makes Spanish seem a more stable language that its predecessors in the Eastern cities. In any case, researchers report no strong influence of Spanish grammar on the English of first-generation Puerto Rican adolescents. Younger children, still under the influence of their parents at four or five, may show a much heavier Spanish overlay in their English.

In those regions of the United States directly bordering on a foreign language area, the situation is different. There are two such regions: Maine, next to French-speaking Quebec, and the Southwest, near Spanish-speaking Mexico. Spanish continues as the native language of children in the Southwest and shows no signs of disappearing. In the same area, there are large numbers of Native American children—Navajo, Apache, Papago and others—for whom English is a second language.

Many more children will have different grammatical systems from their teachers because they speak some nonstandard dialect of English. For these children, English is their first language, but the dialect is different from that of the teacher. There is a general consensus among educated speakers on the grammar of standard English. Disputes are confined to a series of familiar controversies, like *It's me* vs. *It's I,* and a number of fine points which rarely occur in natural speech. But most children differ from their teachers in their use of a number of frequent nonstandard forms which make up a general, subordinate social dialect. Though many teachers may once have used such forms in their own native vernacular, they have learned to avoid them in the course of being educated. For most regions of the United

States, the number of different items involved is surprisingly small: a dozen or so rules, concentrated in the marking of the objective case in pronouns, agreement between third singular subject and verb, irregular forms of the perfect, the comparative and adverbial-*ly*, a few conjunctions, and such well known markers as *ain't*. The persistence of these forms is a tribute to the strength and utility of the nonstandard dialects, rather than any inherent difficulty in converting to the standard rules. More details follow for regional dialects, Creoles, and Black English.

Regional dialects. Some regional dialects differ much more from the standard English of the classroom (SE) than the usual urban nonstandard speech. Rural New England, Appalachia and many regions of the South show nonstandard grammars with striking points of contrast with SE. Southern dialects freely employ negative inversion for emphasis: *Didn't anybody see it* may be a statement in the South, but can only be a question in the North. There are also deeper social differences in the South than elsewhere: *Ain't nobody see it* is the most nonstandard equivalent of the form just given. Most teachers in these areas come from the same region and have an intuitive grasp of these grammatical forms, though not necessarily a full enough understanding to teach the contrasting sets of rules to children.

When a regional dialect is transplanted to another region—usually a rural dialect to an urban region—it typically becomes a subordinate, stigmatized social dialect. This is the case with the speech of Blacks from the rural South who move to the northern cities. The linguistic distance between them and their teachers is greatly increased by this move, so that there is a regional *and* a social barrier. The same is true of Appalachian speakers who move to midwestern cities such as Columbus or Cleveland.

Creole languages. There are two types of English spoken within the borders of the United States which are more different from SE than any of the dialects mentioned, but not as different as the foreign languages French or Spanish. These are Creoles—distinct languages with a largely English vocabulary, not readily intelligible to speakers of SE. Creoles are native languages descended from contact vernaculars or pidgins, reduced forms of language developed when speakers of radically different languages encountered the need for daily communication. One such English Creole is Gullah, spoken in coastal South Carolina and Georgia by Blacks, especially on the Sea Islands. Gullah directly or indirectly influences all of the English spoken in that region. The other is Hawaiian Creole (generally known as "Pidgin" in Hawaii), which is the native language of most of the non-Caucasian population on the islands. Adults and older youth use a modified form of these Creoles in conversation with outsiders, so that many outsiders believe that the Creoles no longer exist as distinct languages. But children coming to school maintain the Creole tradition, and most of them preserve it as their basic vernacular until their early 20s at least. The term "Creole" originally referred to the type of French-based vernacular spoken

Children should be helped to organize themselves into groups with considerable age range, where it is the natural task of the older to explain things to the younger.

in Louisiana, which still has an influence on the speech of children in some areas.

Black English. Black English . . . is a remarkably uniform dialect used by Black children in all of the inner city ghetto areas and throughout most of the South. . . . studies by William Labov (1972), Roger Shuy, William Stewart (1968), Walter Wolfram and others have found that the grammar of Black English (BE) is essentially the same in Boston, New York, Philadelphia, Washington, Cleveland, Detroit, Chicago, St. Louis, New Orleans, San Francisco and Los Angeles. There is evidence that BE has a Creole background—that it has inherited certain grammatical features from an earlier Creole spoken throughout the South, similar to those spoken in the Caribbean, and is itself the product of a language contact situation between European and African languages. BE is therefore the combination of all the differentiating factors mentioned above: it inherits a nonstandard regional dialect, transported to other regions in a subordinate position; a Creolized pattern which is the result of contact with other languages; and shares general nonstandard features of English such as negative concord ("double negatives") and irregular perfects such as *I had came*.

The overall results of Labov's research on BE show that the striking differences from SE heard in the stream of speech are superficial in a linguistic and logical sense. Though BE differs from SE more than any other nonstandard dialect, it is not a foreign language in any sense of the word. The underlying set of meaningful categories are the same, with one or two notable exceptions. The striking differences in surface structures are largely due to (1) the rules for contraction of grammatical particles, (2) phonetic realization of a few sounds, (3) different intonational patterns, and (4) different distribution of a few redundant elements.

The situation with the regular past tense illustrates the general point. Black children often say *He pick me up yesterday* where the word pick seems to have no ending. But careful examination of a number of dialects shows that the rule which produces *pick* is used by all speakers of English to a greater or lesser extent: it is an optional deletion of a phonetic *-t* or *-d* after another consonant. BE carries the *-t, -d* deletion rule further than other dialects, and includes the past tense *-ed* in its scope much more often. But there are no BE speakers who never use *-ed*. The plural *-s* occurs in BE, though there are some few differences in irregular forms such as *deers* in place of *deer*. In contrast, the Creoles based on English have a very different grammatical apparatus. Jamaican Creole has no *-ed* and no plural *-s*. The past tense is usually not marked at all, and the habitual present is marked with a prefix *-a* before the verb. The plural is marked by the suffix *dem: di buk dem* corresponds to SE and BE *the books*. Hawaiian Creole has no *-ed* either, but uses the auxiliary *went* instead: *He went pick em up* for SE *He picked it up*.

Forms of the verb *to be* like *is* and *are* and *were*—together called the "copula"—become even more central in the discussion of the logic of the child as evidenced by his language (Labov 1970). Some psychologists working with preschool children have thought that they lacked the ability to make logical statements because the copula was not present. *They mine* or *He my brother* were taken as illogical expressions. The present tense copula is of course not logically necessary; most languages dispense with it in such sentences. However, in this case, BE is merely extending the contraction rule to drop these forms when they are not emphasized, under the same conditions as govern the SE contractions *They're mine* and *He's my brother.* (BE has in addition an undeletable copula *be* which marks the habitual present.) In any case, we find that all BE speakers have an abstract copula which appears with emphasis or whenever contraction is not permitted, as in *He is my brother* and *That's what he is.* Children four to eight years old use the full form of *is* even more than older children who have mastered the BE vernacular.

Developmental vs. dialect differences

The view of language differences just presented will be complicated in the day care program because many four-year-olds have an incomplete grasp of the grammar and phonetics of their basic dialect, standard or nonstandard. At this age, they often have problems with the articulation of *l* and *r*, so that contracted forms of *will* and *are* in *He'll* and *They're* are particularly elusive. They have difficulty with the sound of *th*, as in *them* or *thin*, and produce instead *t* and *d* or *f* and *v*. They have problems with such consonant clusters as -*st* and *str-* in *passed, test* and *strong*, as well as *thr-* in *throw*. Labov has found that Black or Puerto Rican children share these developmental patterns, and in some cases they coincide with and reinforce the pattern of their nonstandard dialect. We may hear *skr-* for *str-* in *street* from many children; for Black children, this happens to coincide with a regional South Carolina pattern which is often found in the north.

Grammatical patterns also show a certain degree of similarity between nonstandard and early childhood forms. The forms of questions used by very young children often fail to show a reversal of subject and auxiliary with wh- questions: *Can he go?* but *Where he went?* BE speakers seem to favor this pattern longer than speakers of other dialects, though the standard *Where('d) he go?* is more common in the fully formed BE. Hawaiian Creole has no such reversal even in yes-no questions: we have only *He can go?* with a special high falling intonation signalling the question form.

At the age of four, many children show negative concord in their speech: *they don't like nobody,* which coincides with the general nonstandard form. The distinction between subjective and objective forms of pronouns, especially *he* and *him, she* and *her,* is occasionally missing in the speech of young BE speakers who acquire it later in their adolescent years. It is possible that such irregular patterns survive longer among Black children as an inheritance of Creole patterns which do not distinguish subjective or objective, masculine, feminine or neuter. It does not mean that the young child is confused on the notions of male and female.

The fact that many nonstandard forms coincide with the early developmental patterns of children learning standard English has led many people to assume that nonstandard speakers are simply retarded in their verbal development. Their low verbal output in the traditional school environment and limited school performance reinforces this view. But there is an equally large body of facts that show nonstandard dialect as *further* developments—going beyond the standard—and more remote from childhood patterns than SE. Negative inversion or the deletion of the copula are actually additional steps in the development of the langauge. It is therefore incorrect to identify nonstandard language with underdeveloped language, and the teacher or tutor in a day care program must realize that the differences between his speech and the children's speech represent a mixture of developmental and dialectal differences.

Any program for teaching day care center personnel about language differences will have to come to grips with a set of powerful folk beliefs. (See Baratz and Baratz 1970, for more extended discussion.) We can contrast myth with research evidence as we did for language development in Chapter 1.

Myth: Some languages are better than others. Although some people falsely believe, for example, that some Native American languages are little more than a series of grunts and groans, or that standard English is better than Black dialect for abstract thinking, there is no evidence to support such assertions. All languages are inherently equal in the complexity of their basic grammatical and logical structure. All languages have highly structured rules of sound and syntax, and all languages are used for interpersonal and intrapersonal communication. Different cultures vary concerning what are appropriate topics to talk about—for example, people in nontechnological societies spend less time discussing scientific matters than those in technological societies. But any language has the potential to deal with any topic, if the speakers want to introduce or devleop the appropriate vocabulary.

Myth: Some dialects represent bad language usage. As linguists use the term, "dialect" refers simply to the many varieties of a language that, when taken together, make up a language. For example, English has many dialects in the United States and the United Kingdom. Standard English as we know it in the United States merely represents one dialect among many. The fact that it is the official form of the language for conducting the affairs of state, business and education does not mean that (in terms of its linguistic properties) it is any better than white Appalachian dialect, Black nonstandard dialect or Hawaiian Pidgin English. All dialects of a language (including the standard) are systematic, highly structured language codes.

Myth: People who speak a nonstandard dialect are stupid. Following from the myth that dialects are bad is the false conclusion that people who speak nonstandard dialects are necessarily stupid. Such an assumption erroneously assumes that any utterance that is not in standard English is the result of poor learning of standard English rather than the result of good learning of a dialect other than the Standard. The language variety one learns reflects where and with whom one lives, not the intelligence with which one is endowed.

In many instances people who make statements concerning the worthlessness of nonstandard dialects have failed to separate the linguistic reality from the social one. The fact that standard English dialect is important for negotiations in the larger mainstream society, and the fact that the larger mainstream society devalues and distorts the validity of nonstandard dialect does not make the latter any less structured or rule governed in terms of its linguistic features. Such social devaluing indicates how the language myths, maintained by the ignorance and ethnocentrism of the mainstream society, have inadvertently generated prejudice.

Myth: Learning a nonstandard dialect is not learning a language. This leads to the commonly held assumption that children from economically deprived backgrounds are verbally destitute. Educators and psychologists in their ignorance concerning language learning and language usage have contributed greatly to creating and maintaining the "verbal underdevelopment" myth. Such a myth arose because these educators erroneously equated being verbal with being proficient in standard English—thus confusing nonstandard utterances with "underdeveloped" language.

In addition, in many experiments designed by these educators to elicit language, they not only used stimuli which were linguistically biased in favor of standard English, but also violated social conventions of the very children that they tested. Language learning involves not only acquiring the rules of the structure of the dialect but also the social conventions of its usage, i.e., what topics are talked about, with whom one talks, etc. In certain cultures, it is inappropriate behavior for a child to make a "display" of his knowledge to an adult even if the elder happens to be kind—the proverbial friendly white examiner. The Black child's *I 'on' know* may more often reflect his perception of the alien social situation than his ignorance.

The prevalence of these myths among teachers may be related to their own social background. According to one estimation, 80 percent of teachers come from the middle class, and a good proportion of this percentage comes from the lower middle class. This is the group which Labov has found frequently the most linguistically insecure. No comparable estimate is available for day care personnel, but the presence of large numbers of paraprofessionals may make the problem of adult insecurity about language even greater. People who are themselves insecure may become rigid and hostile when children display speech patterns which they hate in themselves.

Unfortunately, these folk beliefs about language differences are more damaging to a good day care program than folk beliefs about how language develops. We now realize that the expectations which a teacher has for his children will influence how he teaches and how much his children learn. There is mounting evidence that one of the most important cues a teacher responds to in developing these expectations is his children's speech. Frederick Williams (in Chicago) and Wayne Shamo (in Memphis) found that teachers evaluate children more negatively when their speech has nonstandard pronunciation and syntax. Judith Guskin (in Ann Arbor) found that teachers-in-training rated Black speakers as less likely to succeed academically than white speakers. Seligman, Tucker and Lambert (in Montreal) found that a recorded speech pattern or a child's photograph carried more weight than the quality of a child's composition or drawing in third grade teachers' ratings. There is no reason to believe that preschool teachers, in-service or preservice, would be less susceptible to these prejudiced reactions. Monica Holmes and Douglas Holmes compared the evaluations of a Head Start teacher (in Coney Island) with observations and IQ tests of the children in her class. The teacher's ratings of her children's intelligence were not correlated with actual intelligence test scores, and they were biased by such actual behaviors as the child's willingness to respond to directions and his general verbal skills.

We do not know how a training program for teachers should be designed to deal with such ethnocentric biases. Since these reactions are deeply founded in the teachers' own past experiences, they probably will not be changed merely by learning the facts of language differences.

Differences in verbal styles

Children differ markedly in their strategies for learning. (1) Some make every bit of new knowledge explicit and insist on repeating aloud everything they know. (2) Others store up knowledge like blotters, rarely producing it even on demand. (3) Others avoid new learning and insulate themselves from it as much as possible. The difference between these strategies or individual styles is crucial in planning a successful program.

It has been considered the task of teachers to diagnose such individual differences in behavior. No test now in use seems to differentiate children who are following path (2) from those who follow (3). But certain general sociolinguistic principles operate beyond the influence of individual personalities. There are striking differences in the way that children talk to each other and the way they talk in the presence of adults. Oldest children or only children show fastest verbal development, and more of it, in the sense of strategy (1) above. Practice in communication with adults leads to more explicit verbalization, better performance on reading readiness tests, better initial performance in school. The conclusion of most teachers is that the more silent children lack the necessary requirements for verbal development—contact with adult speakers of SE—and need more individual attention from the teacher, even one-to-one tutoring.

Some children do indeed talk more fluently to adults. But empirical studies show that many children talk less with adults than with their peers. Their responses to adults may also be less complex than the kind of speech they produce among themselves. Children who are tagged as "nonverbal" in test situations with an adult often show remarkable verbal skills when adults are absent. This is particularly true among Black and Puerto Rican children who have a highly developed verbal culture of their own which is not easily accepted or appreciated by parents and teachers. Teachers will need to be imaginative in trying a variety of methods for adapting to individual differences in verbal style.

Teachers often want to obtain samples of children's language, either for evaluation or for instruction—as in creating experience charts for beginning reading. To obtain such language, teachers often use the same technique as testers: ask the child to tell a story about a picture. The following examples are taken from such a teacher-tester situation, where the most elaborate language elicited consists of such simple, unconnected sentences as: *The girl got a bike. . . . The boy's playin' football.* In the typical exchange, the adult does most of the talking:

Teacher: Where are they playing, James?
James: On the street.
Teacher: Do you think the street's a good place to play in?
James: Yes.
Teacher: You do? All right, go ahead. Tell me some more. Why do you think it is a good place to play in?
James: 'Cause they like to play.

The main sociolinguistic control upon speech is the unequal power relation between adult and child. No matter what demands are made upon the child, no matter how obscure and pointless the questions may seem, he is obliged to answer. The typical reaction of many preschool children is to give minimal responses, sometimes the exact reverse of the answer the adult is demanding. This happens most often when the adult combines moral instruction with his inquiry, and thus confuses the roles of preacher and teacher.

Teacher: Mays, do you see all that paper in the street?
Mays: Yeah.
Teacher: How do you think it got there?
Mays: It blew there.
Teacher: Do you think that children could do anything to help keep the street clean?
Mays: Nah.

The tendency to act as an agent of social improvement is a difficult one to resist even in the midst of an exploration of the child's verbal skills. Day care programs are particularly apt to develop this line of adult-child relationship, since many adults think their primary responsibility lies in keeping the child out of trouble and improving his social behavior. In any case, the adult should recognize that he will provoke in many children the defensive behavior illustrated above. Many educational programs are based upon such false evidence of the child's restricted verbal capacity and are devoted to the task of providing him with a "new language." Teachers and supervisors should recognize this monosyllabic behavior as evidence of the restricted school environment which produces it. The first step in extending each child's verbal abilities is to create a school setting which stimulates each child to use all the langauge he has.

Language in the day care center

In the day care center, children can talk to other children and to adults. It is important to make maximum use of all these human resources. Following are two sections on talk among children and adult-child talk. We end with two shorter postscripts on selecting a language as the medium of communication in the day care center, and a suggestion for cultural pluralism in the curriculum.

Talk among children

We have said above that children in most day care center populations will use their fullest grammatical skills when talking to other children. This means, as a minimum, that centers should encourage as much talk among children in school as would normally occur outside. Ideally, more can be done to maximize the benefits of child talk for each participant. Three functions of speech seem particularly important as incentives for complex language.

Speech for self-aggrandizement. The primary factor here is power relations. The most language is produced when there is no one present of superior status: in other words, when nothing the child says can be held against him. It is even helpful to have someone of clearly inferior status present, an argument for mixed-age grouping. One of the major uses of language is self-aggrandizement with respect to others: raising one's own status and lowering theirs. Children use the system of adult norms as an instrument for this purpose and become involved in complex propositions on the future consequences of present or future acts. To illustrate this point, we can use extracts from the free conversation of the same six-year-old quoted above. Those present are James, his close friend Mays, a smaller and younger boy named Harold and a rabbit.

Mays: James, I told you not to move with him no more! If he fall out your lap and hurt hisself, that's your fault an' you gonna pay for it! . . .
James: You better sit back down, boy, before he get ma-ad, and beat you up for some carrots.

Language for explication. A second major incentive for complex language is the need for explication: as in puzzling out the complex workings of machinery:

Mays: Look at it, look at—that's why it's turnin' around. You know why it's turnin' around? 'Cause makin' that thing. . . .
The first two functions are combined in:
Mays: How can a bunny rabbit talk to *you*! He only don't even know how to speak!

Language for aesthetic pleasure. The third motivating factor for complex speech is *aesthetic*. Children play with syntax as well as sound, and can demonstrate skills which go far beyond any current program of instruction.

The following example combines the aesthetic and the normative functions of language:

James: The more he get nervous—
Mays: —the more he gonna jump off!
James: Uh-uh. The more he get nervous, the more he die, the more Harold gonna hafta pay the *doctor* bills!
Mays: Right. 'N' the more he get nervous. . . .
James: Tck! The more he die, the more Harold gonna hafta pay the doctor bills.

The linguistic skills of these children are beyond the school program which is being offered them. The task of the day care program, if it is to be successful, is to draw upon the energy and versatility displayed here for constructive ends. This can be done by constructing social situations in which these abilities naturally come into play. Children should be helped to organize themselves into groups with considerable age range, where it is the natural task of the older to explain things to the younger (and where the younger is not necessarily degraded for not knowing something). Also they should have available objects of considerable mechanical complexity, where their desire for explication can be given full scope.

Many day care programs use puppet plays and other role-playing situations to stimulate language. This can be a successful device if three basic relationships are incorporated. Adults should provide roles and situations, but not model behavior or the plot. Characters can be constructed who are in an inferior role in relation to the children—puppets, animals or robots who know less than the children themselves. Objects and settings for such roles can be complicated up to the point where it is possible for any small child to get lost in them.

These suggestions for maximizing the value of talk among children come from sociolinguistic analyses of children's spontaneous speech. They are important because so often in discussions of programs for young children the impression is given that planning for one-to-one talk between adult and child is all that matters. Hopefully, we can learn more about how to create conditions for complex talk among children by analyzing what happens when these ideas are tried out. Whatever situations are most likely to elicit a child's most complex language are also useful contexts for diagnosing his growth in verbal abilities over time.

Adult-child talk

Adults can talk to children in ways which are uniquely beneficial to their language and cognitive development, and day care centers should be operated to maximize the effectiveness of adult resources. But what counts is the quality of adult-child talk, not just the quantity, and the organizational conditions in which high quality talk is most likely to occur.

Quality of talk. The first major step is to shift the role and behavior of the adult away from that of interviewer to that of a resource for the child to draw upon. Unfortunately, many language curricula depend largely on question-answer sequences. Questions put by the adult should be true requests for information, rather than know-answer questions of requests for display. To the extent that an adult takes on the role of disciplinarian, he can hardly serve as the center of a free exchange of ideas.

Barbara Tizard and Jack Tizard (Tizard, Cooperman, Joseph, and Tizard 1972) have studied the conditions in residential nurseries in Great Britain which promote language development [see Chapter 2]. They found that " 'informative' remarks by the staff tended to evoke a response in the children, while commands and 'time passing' remarks did not. The more frequent the prohibition in an adult's talk, the less often was she answered by the children."

Surprising as it may seem, many adults need help in learning how to talk to children in productive ways. Greenberg (1970) reports on a workshop session from the Child Development Group of Mississippi:

> *Talking* about talking with children didn't work. If people don't habitually talk lengthily with children, they don't know *how* to talk lengthily with children. So we actually practiced it:
>
> **Tape plays:**
> **Teacher:** Oh, you tease, Tom, what are you telling Winston?
> **Tom:** I tellin' him my brother Gary a bad bad boy.
> **Teacher:** Oh, now that ain't nice.
>
> The group analyzes and discusses this. Then the same teacher goes to find Tom, who is waiting for our staff meeting to be over so one of the teachers will drive him home. The same teacher runs through the same conversation. I tape this conversation too, and afterward we discuss it to see if and how the teacher prolonged and enriched the verbal exchange.
>
> **Teacher:** Tom, what was you tellin' Winston this mornin' when you was playin' with the ball?
> **Tom:** I tole him Gary my brother.
> **Teacher:** You like Gary?
> **Tom:** Yeah, I lahk him, but he bad.
> . . . (three Teacher-Tom interchanges)
> **Teacher:** Why's dat?
> **Tom:** 'Cause he walked up and set with his friend when they was singin' 'bout Jesus and the preacher was preachin'.
> **Teacher:** Who whipped him?
> **Tom:** Daddy—he tuk him outside and whupped him with a red belt.
> **Teacher:** Did Gary cry?
> **Tom:** Oh, yeah, he got tears in his eyes. Mama wiped his eyes with a rag when he come back in. Then he popped his fingers. That boy can't *never* be quiet.
> . . . (and so on for at least five more Teacher-Tom interchanges). (1969, pp. 165-166)

In the above conversation, adult and child are talking about a past event.

Sometimes it may be easier to engage a child in extended conversation about some object actually present. David Hawkins (a philosopher of science) relates how he learned from his wife Frances (a nursery school teacher) how to talk with small children:

> I learned . . . that one of the very important factors in this kind of situation is that there be some third thing which is of interest to the child and to the adult, in which they can join in outward projection. Only this creates a possible stable bond of communication, of shared concern. . . . So the first act in teaching, it seems to me, the first goal necessary to all others, is to encourage this kind of engrossment. Then the child comes alive for the teacher as well as the teacher for the child. They have a common engrossment for discussion, they are involved together in the world. (1967, p. 7)

In these conversations, teachers should try (even at the risk of initial self-consciousness) to use elaborated and precise language themselves (within the limit of the child's comprehension). There is evidence that the elaboration of teacher talk is reflected in the talk of their children (Smothergill, Olson, and Moore 1971), and that it is the quality of talk, not the quantity, that counts (Tizard, Cooperman, Joseph, and Tizard 1972). McAfee (1967) gives suggestions for vocabulary, and Lavatelli (1971, pp. 112-118) includes suggestions for syntax prepared by two psycholinguists, Ursula Bellugi and Wilbur Hass.

Finally, the reinforcing nature of the affective relationship between child and adult can be used deliberately to facilitate learning in the child. When a warm and trusting relationship between the two has developed, games and other forms of play may serve as a context for learning. But for maximum effect, the child must learn that from the games the teacher will expect some response. Just as there is a difference for an adult between reading a detective story for his own satisfaction and reading a drivers' license manual to pass an examination, so there is a difference between play for play's sake and play designed to provoke responses from the child in a context of learning. If the child learns that the blocks or toys with which he is playing are related to a response the teacher will expect of him, he seems to learn to process the experiences he has in a more systematic manner. This ability to organize information with the purpose of an eventual response to an adult or peer is probably most efficiently learned in the one-to-one situation between adult and child where the adult can, with smiles, nods and words of encouragement, reinforce the child's responses which order the materials he is playing with. Organizing information for response to others is an essential characteristic of most human intellective abilities, no matter how one wishes to define intelligence.

Organizational conditions. The Tizards' research points to organizational conditions in day care centers which probably will affect how often high quality conversations take place between adults and children. The adult-child ratio is not the only factor, though that is important. They found that nurseries in which the children's language development was highest were also characterized by a smaller proportion of children under three, greater staff stability and greater staff autonomy. Where the proportion of very young children was high, the staff was preoccupied with the burdens of physical care. Where the staff turnover was high, the adults were less apt to understand the early speech of the young child. Where staff autonomy was low, the adult saw her job more as "'minding' the children under the eye of her supervisor." Finally, within any given adult-child ratio, conversation may depend on how staff responsibilities are allocated. The Tizards found that "when two staff were on duty with a group of six children, the junior of the two tended to talk less and interact less with the children than when she was alone in charge of the group." Adults as well as children are influenced by the power relations inherent in speech situations. We need more studies like the Tizards' of how features of complex organizations influence behavior and thereby affect the child's development.

Which language to use

Day care programs must take into account that most of the children have limited command of standard English. The basic approach used in the past has been the "sink or swim" method, where foreign language speakers or BE speakers were confronted with an SE speaking classroom. Children have a surprising ability to cope with such an abrupt switch. Experiments in Quebec show that English-speaking middle class children can accept a totally French-speaking school without any obvious problems. But this is under the most favorable circumstances. The obvious fact remains that BE-, Creole-, French-, Spanish- or Indian-speaking children do not take full advantage of the English-speaking schools, and their overall educational achievement is very low. From all indications, the low performance of Black, Hispanic, or Native American children is the result of general cultural factors. But while the absence of their native language from the classroom may not present insuperable cognitive obstacles, it may be decisive in defining the school or preschool as an alien and hostile environment.

It follows that ideally both the children's native language or dialect and standard English should be used in the classroom. How much English and how much of the other language is an open question. A further and more difficult question concerns the selection of day care personnel—whether staff for a center or mothers for home day care. Which is more important: fluency in the child's native language or some degree of fluency in standard English? As certification requirements for educational personnel change from academic degrees to performance criteria, the question of criteria in language becomes important.

Obviously the best qualified adult would be fluent in all languages and dialects represented, but the supply of such multilingual experts is extremely limited. Answers to these questions will depend on the attitudes and goals of the parents, on the availability of bilingual personnel and on more knowledge than we now have of how best to teach children a second dialect or language in a school setting while promoting their fluency in their first language as well. (See Dodson, Price, and Williams [1968]; John and Horner [1971] for discussions of bilingual programs for young children.)

Teaching cultural pluralism

We assume a goal of cultural pluralism—many different ethnic groups living together, sharing and borrowing while retaining their ethnic distinctiveness. The early childhood day care center offers a unique opportunity for children to learn about their own cultural identity while learning at the same time to respect others. A curriculum for young children can be designed so that they can learn not only about the language, culture and mores of their own group or of mainstream America but also of the many distinct ethnic groups that are a part of the American society. More materials are becoming available that can be used for the intercultural education of young children.

Food is a topic dear to all children, and exploration of the food tastes of varied ethnic groups could provide an excellent beginning for learning about cultural differences. It should not be difficult, especially in urban areas, for teachers to obtain samples of the foods of Jews, Italians, Blacks, Poles, Chinese, Mexican-Americans, etc., from neighborhood stores. Information on songs, dances, games and the social customs of children from different cultures are available from such sources as Folkways Records, the United Nations Educational, Scientific and Cultural Organization and many ethnic organizations such as B'nai B'rith, the Knights of Columbus and the National Association for the Advancement of Colored People.

In using all these materials it is important that they be related to what the children already know. It will not help for a white child in Los Angeles to learn wonderful things about Pedro in Seville while he remains contemptuous of José in the inner city of Los Angeles, nor to admire Aki the Nigerian boy while he considers Leroy ignorant because he says *"ain't."* By the same token, it seems at best devious, and perhaps futile as well, to teach a lower socioeconomic class American Black child to respect himself by learning to respect tribal Africans on the one hand, or middle class American . . . [Blacks] on the other. The kind of identity which the lower socioeconomic class American . . . [Black] child must learn to respect is his own—including his own variety of walking style, dress and language.

Undoubtedly, the most important resource is the variety of backgrounds within the day care center itself. Language differences among children and staff—and cultural differences of all kinds—should be welcomed, openly discussed and used in the curriculum. Hopefully, adults as well as children will gain greater self-confidence in themselves and more realistic attitudes towards others.

References

Baratz, S. S., and Baratz, J. C. "Early Childhood Intervention: The Social Science Base of Institutional Racism." *Harvard Educational Review* 40 (1970): 29-50.

Dodson, C. J.; Price, E.; and Williams, I. *Towards Bilingualism: Studies in Language Teaching Methods.* Cardiff: University of Wales Press, 1968.

Greenberg, P. *The Devil Has Slippery Shoes: A Biased Biography of the Child Development Group of Mississippi.* New York: Macmillan, 1970.

Hawkins, D. I. "Thou It." Paper presented at Primary Teachers' Residential Course, Leicestershire, England, April 1967.

John, V. P., and Horner, V. *Early Childhood Bilingual Education.* New York: Modern Language Association, 1971.

Labov, W. *Language in the Inner City.* Philadelphia: University of Pennsylvania Press, 1972.

Labov, W. "The Logic of Nonstandard English." In *Language and Poverty: Perspectives on a Theme,* ed. F. Williams. Chicago: Markham, 1970.

Lavatelli, C. S., ed. *Language Training in Early Childhood Education.* Urbana: University of Illinois Press for the ERIC Clearinghouse on Early Childhood Education, 1971.

*McAfee, O. "The Right Words." *Young Children* 23, no. 2 (November 1967): 74-78.

Palmer, F. H. "Socioeconomic Status and Intellective Performance Among Negro Preschool Boys." *Developmental Psychology* 3 (1970): 1-9.

Smothergill, N. L.; Olson, F.; and Moore, S. G. "The Effects of Manipulation of Teacher Communication Style in the Preschool." *Child Development* 42 (1971): 1229-1239.

Stewart, W. "Continuity and Change in American Negro Dialects." *Florida Foreign Language Reporter* 6, no. 1.3 (1968).

Tizard, B.; Cooperman, O.; Joseph, A.; and Tizard, J. "Environmental Effects on Language Development: A Study of Young Children in Long-Stay Residential Nurseries." *Child Development* 43 (1972): 337-358.

The best way to make the student comfortable when speaking the target language is to establish a language relationship in that language from the beginning.

Janet Gonzalez-Mena

9.
English As a
Second Language for
Preschool Children

English as a second language (ESL) programs sometimes leave much to be desired. Many seem to be designed for efficiency, assuming that language is something that can be lifted out of life (out of context) and instilled in a child. Language acquisition, however, particularly in preschool-age children, is a very complex mixture of inherent linguistic and cognitive phenomena, developing within a constantly changing situational context. Greater understanding is needed of some of the more important aspects of second-language learning in the young child.

Any second-language program for young children should be based on the following principles:

1. Children are motivated to learn a second language because of language relationships.
2. Young children need a total development program within a language program.
3. Children learn by doing.

Establishing a language relationship

The first problem confronting any foreign-language teacher is how to get the students to speak the target language. A three- or four-year-old child does not have the motivation of an adult who is leaving for Spain in six months and is enrolled in a Spanish class. After all, the child has a means of communicating that is comfortable and familiar. Why would any child want to struggle to learn another language? The answer is simple. Young children will struggle; in fact, they will put forth great effort, *if* they

---

feel a need. How can a teacher help the children feel a need? The teacher can establish an English-language relationship with each child.

Many teachers of ESL say over and over to their children, "Speak English! Speak English!" They may even explain in the child's native tongue why it is important to learn English. All this becomes unnecessary with the establishment of an English-language relationship between teacher and child, and undue frustration will be largely eliminated.

The concept of language relationships can be easily observed in anyone who speaks more than one language. Perhaps an example would best explain it. Juan came to California from Mexico ten years ago. He and his wife always speak Spanish to each other although both have learned English. Juan also speaks Spanish to his good friend, Jaime, but to Jaime's wife he speaks English because she was born in Texas. Although she speaks Spanish fluently, she is shy about it because people from Mexico have laughed at her accent and vocabulary. Juan is taking an English class. During the coffee break (when the language relationships become obvious), he speaks Spanish to Luis, who is from Chile. He speaks English to Pierre, a fellow student from France. At the restaurant where he works, he speaks English with the cook, an Anglo, and Spanish with the waiter, a teenager recently arrived from Mexico.

Juan does not have to make decisions about which language to speak—it is an automatic reaction. If he speaks English with someone with whom he has a Spanish-language relationship, he may very likely feel strange and uncomfortable. Language teachers need to know about this feeling. Better yet—they should have experienced this feeling themselves.

Every effort should be made to minimize such a linguistically-induced, negative psychological state in the students, whether adult or child. The best way to make the student comfortable when speaking the target language is to establish a language relationship in that language from the beginning.

My own experiences have convinced me of the importance of the language relationship in motivating the child. I have found that the children identify me as an English-speaking person who speaks Spanish. At first, totally monolingual children say everything to me in Spanish, but as they develop English skills they begin to utilize the English they know, using Spanish only to supplement what they cannot yet express. I have not had to say, "Speak English," because children try to use all the English they know when speaking with me. This would not be true if I tried to teach English using Spanish as the vehicle. I have heard teachers do this: "Dime *car*." ("Say *car* for me.") Unfortunately, to communicate with this teacher, the child will use Spanish, saving English for the English lesson. There is more than one way to handle this problem of two languages. The method of separating the languages by teachers is but one of several approaches. See Andersson and Boyer (1970) for a typology of bilingual education.

The issue of ESL-only versus ESL as part of bilingual education must be confronted. In the ESL-only approach, children may have no adult in school with whom to have a native-language relationship. However, this two-way linguistic thrust is needed if they are to continue to grow and develop in their native language. Otherwise, the children either speak English entirely, or use English exclusively for thinking, logical and intellectual processes, keeping the native language for their homes. These children do not become true bilingual speakers because they acquire no words, tools, or skills for higher thinking in their own native language (Manuel 1965).

The above is one of several strong arguments in favor of bilingual education as opposed to only ESL. The United States needs truly bilingual adults, and our education system has not only failed to produce bilinguals, but has actually discouraged the development of the native language in children who began school speaking a language other than English.

Moreover, a bilingual program tends to have a positive effect on the educational longevity of low-income children whose dominant language is other than English. Many of these children fall behind in school and eventually drop out (Andersson and Boyer 1970). The proponents of bilingual education believe that the child's first language and the child's self-esteem are so tied together that they cannot be separated. If the native language of the child is replaced by English (which very often happens), it is as if to say that the child's native language is not as good nor useful. Because language is an integral part of personality, any affront to language is a blow to self-esteem (Cohen 1970).

The young child who has not yet developed in the area of language, who is still in the process of incorporating the internal structure of a first language, should not be hindered in that development. In other words, if growth in the first language is cut off in midstream, the child may be left floundering in a new language. Research indicated that children who are secure in the development of their first language acquire a second language faster and better (John and Horner 1971).

Children need a total development program

Young children are not only in the midst of their language development, but also in the midst of their total development. They are forming concepts (which may or may not be considered as separate from language) and acquiring other cognitive skills such as problem solving. Children are learning to interpret the messages from the five senses and are developing perceptual skills. They are, of course, also developing motor skills (which can be tied to perceptions and called perceptual-motor skills). For the adult, one of these areas may be isolated and taught separately—such as language. Isolating one skill from the others would be doing the child a disservice because they are so closely tied into one another, if not inseparable.

For example, suppose your objective as an ESL teacher is to teach the English word for *triangle*. To adult students you have to do nothing more than draw one, and tell them "triangle." You could also mention the native language word for it (although language interference might result if the word is similar, e.g., if you say "triangulo" and "triangle" together for the Spanish speakers, they may say "tree-angle" or "try-angoolo"). But little else is usually necessary. The point is—the adult has the concept; all that is needed is the English label for it.

However, young children may not have the concept or the label in any language. In fact, they may not even be able to perceive a triangle as yet; they may see no difference between a square and a triangle. They may feel no difference if given a block with three corners or one with four corners. What young children need are many experiences with triangles while acquiring the label. They need to make triangles with crayons and clay, fit them together as in playing with puzzles and blocks, touch, manipulate them . . . even eat them (as in one-half of a sandwich). Then when a label is attached, the children have experiences upon which to base the concept. If a label is given to a piece of paper cut with three corners, how do children know whether or not the paper is the defining characteristic, or the color, weight, or size? Children *build* the concept "triangle"—it is not instilled in them. Once they understand the concept, they have little difficulty labeling or using two labels such as triangle and triangulo.

Children learn by doing

The above example also illustrates the third principle necessary for an early childhood ESL program: Children learn by doing. How else can children gain experiences as a basis for language development? They can explore, experiment, find out for themselves. Piaget's work indicated that the child needs "active, self-discovery, inductively oriented learning experiences whereby . . . [the child] is able to perform transformations on materials from the environment (Evans 1971, p. 235)." Only after performing physical actions on physical objects can children then move to mental action on objects. Learning is interacting with the environment, not remaining passive and being told about it. If this assumption is basic, the ESL teacher will not hold up a picture of a ball and say, "Repeat after me, 'This is a ball.' " Yes, the adult can get children to react to a picture of a ball with "This is a ball." But unless children have concrete experiences such as rolling balls, sucking on a jawbreaker, or making snowballs, they are just parroting. They are like machines spitting out that which has been programmed.

We acquire meanings to words through their connotations, not their denotations. Connotations consist of all the feelings, verbal and nonverbal, that surround a word (and are different for each person), while denotations are the definitions of the word. Holt (1969) stated that he has a vocabulary of about 25,000 words, yet he has probably looked up fewer than 50 words in the dictionary in his life. He gained the denotations from the connotations which were derived from his personal experiences. "Language is caught, not taught" would seem to be a good motto for ESL teachers.

Learning is interacting with the environment, not remaining passive and being told about it.

Additionally, the social development of children cannot be ignored, or children will be greatly hampered in other developmental areas. I would suggest that social development and ESL be tied together by insuring social interaction between the ESL child and other children who speak English. Moreover a program based on the assumptions and principles described here will provide opportunities for social interaction which may strengthen social growth and development.

Summary

The adults in a foreign-language class already have achieved full language development. The job of the teacher is to work around any inhibitions and help the students acquire a second language (or third or fourth). What the teacher does in the classroom probably has little effect on the students' native language(s) except perhaps to add some insights.

Conversely, young children are in the midst of their development—not only in language, but also in conceptual growth, cognitive skills, perceptual-motor development, etc. Furthermore, children have not built up the walls of inhibitions to protect themselves psychologically. They are eager to learn, and their mistakes can help them learn. Young children have been experimenting with sounds since they were born and in most cases are more than willing to continue trying. What children need are the opportunities to hear and use the target language; it does not need to be "dragged out" of them. Young children do not need to be motivated. As long as children speak with a person with whom they have an English-language relationship, they are most willing to speak English. A child who is asked to play cars by two English-speaking friends is going to speak English with them. No one needs to stand over the children and remind them to speak English.

In too many programs the total focus is on the level of achievement in language skills. We teach and evaluate in the cognitive area, completely skipping over the affective aspects. How does each child feel about this new skill and the culture to which it is tied? That is a question that should be asked. How did the child feel about her or his native language upon entrance to the ESL program? Have the child's feelings about this native language changed? Has the native language taken a backseat position in the child's life? Evaluating the affective domain is difficult, but it is no less important than the cognitive domain (Nida 1965).

Educators must recognize the value of the wholeness of experience (Holt 1969; Hymes 1968). The world should not be broken up into little pieces, taken apart, called by different subject names, and taught for 15 minutes at a time. When the world is artificially broken into segments, it is difficult for children to put it back together again as a whole. Children can live an entire experience in a second as well as a first language. They take in what they can handle at one time, and that which begins to make sense. They learn by being immersed in the experience rather than having it broken up into little pieces. The teacher's function is to provide experiences which enable children to learn. Children learn language best in real situations with concrete experiences.

References

Andersson, T., and Boyer, M. *Bilingual Schooling in the United States.* Austin, Tex.: Southwest Educational Development Laboratory, 1970.

Cohen, A. *Points of Interest about Bilingual Education with Specific Reference to the Spanish Speaking of the Southwest,* 1970.

Evans, E. D. *Contemporary Influences in Early Childhood Education.* New York: Holt, Rhinehart & Winston, 1971.

Holt, J. *The Underachieving School.* New York: Pitman, 1969.

Hymes, J. L. *Teaching the Child Under Six.* Columbus, Ohio: Merrill, 1968.

John, V. P., and Horner, V. M. *Early Childhood Bilingual Education.* New York: Modern Language Association of America, 1971.

Manuel, H. *Spanish-Speaking Children of the Southwest: Their Education and the Public Welfare.* Austin, Tex.: University of Texas Press, 1965.

Nida, E. A. "Some Psychological Problems in Second Language Learning." In *Teaching English as a Second Language,* ed. H. B. Allen. New York: McGraw-Hill, 1965.

Part III
Language and Reading

Courtney B. Cazden

10.
Language and
Learning to Read

All parents and teachers of young children want to help their children become successful readers. The most important kind of help is to support children's language development in all the ways suggested in this book. But we can help children become readers in more special ways too: reading to children, valuing their play with language, and encouraging them to write. I will elaborate on the first two; in Chapter 11 Chomsky writes about the third.

Reading to children

As Schickedanz pointed out, "children who learn to read easily in school are the same children whose parents have read to them at home (1978, p. 48)." There are several reasons why this is probably not a coincidence, and why teachers should read to children at school.

First, *all children should be familiar with the language of books before they try to read.* For children whose native language is not English, this argues for teaching beginning reading in the child's native language. For all children, it argues for a recognition that the language of books is different from the language of speech.

For example, I heard a preschool teacher reading a book about worms to a small group of children who had just found a large worm on the playground. One passage read: "The worm's mouth is at the fat end. The worm's tail is at the thin end." Had the teacher been talking instead of reading, the children probably would have heard something like this: "The mouth is here [teacher points], and the tail is here," [teacher points again]. Children's books also include unusual idiomatic expressions. For instance, another book about a worm was based on the use of the worm's body as a unit of measurement; it ended with the sentence, "He measured and measured, inch by inch, till he inched out of sight (Lionni 1960)."

In short, the language of books is often not a written version of speech patterns the child already knows. One way in which to match the language of books and speech is the use of each child's individually chosen words and sentences as the first reading material. But eventually children must go beyond their own words and speech pattern and become familiar with the language of books. This will happen most easily if children hear stories read aloud.

Second, *looking at a book together creates an ideal setting for talking about the pictures and the text.* As we mentioned in Chapter 8, not all adults find it easy to talk to children in informative, nondisciplinary ways. Enjoying a book together can be an easy way to begin. Children often ask valuable questions—about something in a picture or what a word means, as Tizard reports in Chapter 2. If the adult asks questions—"Who's that?" or "What's she doing?" or "What do you think will happen next?"—it doesn't seem like interrogation. Children and adults both get pleasure from such demonstrations of what the child has learned.

Sometimes books seem strange to some children because the words do sound different from conversation. In his autobiography, *The Words* (1964), Sartre describes his first encounter with a book version of a story his mother had told him many times in the bath. Her face and her voice were different, and there was no familiar smell of soap surrounding the strange sounding words:

> Ann Marie [his mother] sat me down opposite her, on my little chair. She bent forward, lowered her eyelids, fell asleep. From that statue-like face came a plaster voice. I was bewildered: who was telling what and to whom? My mother had gone off: not a smile, not a sign of complicity. I was in exile. And besides, I didn't recognize her speech . . . A moment later, I realized: it was the book that was speaking. Frightening sentences emerged from it: they were real centipedes. . . . Sometimes they disappeared before I was able to understand them; and other times I understood in advance; and they continued to roll nobly to their end without sparing me a single comma. That discourse was certainly not meant for me.

Eventually Sartre came to love the way books speak, as almost all children do, especially because books make it possible to hear the very same words again and again.

> After a while, I took pleasure in that sudden lift which took me out of myself . . . I grew sensitive to the rigorous succession of words. At each reading, they returned, always the same and in the same order. I awaited them. (1964, pp. 28-29)

Story time has always been highly valued in preschool programs. Teachers should not let pressures from other parts of the program intrude on this experience, especially for children who are not apt to be read to at home. Read to one child on your lap—to a few children on the rug at your feet, or to the whole group—whatever provides the most relaxed concentration for adult and children. Just read.

Teachers should not let pressures from other parts of the program intrude on time for reading stories to children.

Play with language*

So far, all the language we have talked about in this book is for actual communication—about feelings, ideas, and events. What we intuitively know as users of language is also true for children: when either speaking or listening, we are attentive to the meaning, the intention of what we or someone else is trying to say. The language forms are themselves transparent: we hear through them to the meaning itself, and that is the way it should be. As the Duchess rightly says in *Alice in Wonderland:*

. . . the moral of *that* is—take care of the sense and the sounds will take care of themselves.

But aside from normal communication, we enjoy focusing our attention on aspects of language forms themselves—in crossword puzzles and puns, for example. Children do too, as their development proceeds. Metalinguistic awareness, the ability to make the usually transparent forms opaque and to focus on them, is a special kind of language performance, one which makes special cognitive demands, and seems to be less easily acquired than speaking and listening. Our concern as teachers with metalinguistic awareness comes from increasing arguments that it is at least very helpful, and may be critically important in learning to read (Cazden 1975).

Some children seem to be able to think about sounds and words very easily. Everett was a tiny first grader in an inner-city school in San Diego where I was teaching a few years ago (Cazden 1976). His excess energy often erupted in cartwheels across the room, yet he could also sit quietly and reflect on words in a husky whisper: "*Little* is a big word, and *big* is a little word." Seeing *on* written on the blackboard, he said " 'You take the *n* off *on* and put it in front and it'd be *no*.' " Another time, while reading, he came to *w-h-a-t* and asked, " 'What's this word?' " I told him "*what*" and he laughed— " 'When I asked you '*What's this word,*' I said it myself!' "

But other children have more trouble. Venita was a child in a pre-first-grade inner-city summer school in Boston in which children were encouraged to write sentences, with whatever help they needed, about their own experiences. Venita said aloud a fine sentence about a boat trip her family had taken: "The boat can go very fast." However she only wrote down *boat go fast.* When I reminded her what her entire sentence had been, she became confused about where the extra words should have been included. Even though she was actually saying six words, she seemed to be aware only of three. Giving her all the words in her own sentence on large pieces of paper and letting her assemble them herself seemed to help. It was a scrambled word game with her own words.

Playful contexts seem to be particularly useful for learning to think about language forms. Many children spontaneously do play with language by themselves. Sometimes it happens when a very young child is alone in a crib

---

* I am grateful to Ruth Black and Denise Wolf for many conversations on the role of play in the development of symbolic systems.

(Weir 1962; Black 1979).

In her introduction to the reissue of Johnson's book, *Children in "The Nursery School"* (1972), Biber emphasized that Johnson thought that "learning was soundest when the environment encouraged the child in his impulse to 'experiment' with the exercise of his growing powers in the widening world of experience (p. xi)," and she specifically included words as important objects for that experimentation. For example, Georgie, who at 24 months had a fair vocabulary, accompanied motoric activities with varied syllabication:

> As he ran: Bee, bee, bee; Lee, lee, lee; Dub, dub, dub
> At top of slide: Ma-wee, ma-wee, ma-wee, ma-wee, A-a. (p. 254)

Or Matthew, as he was being undressed:

> Nolly lolly, nolly lolly, nilly lolly, sillie Billie, nolly lolly. (p. 255)

And Donald as he ran around the roof:

> Up a lup a dup, Up a dup I go. (p. 256)

Because Johnson's children had companions in their play, as children in their crib do not, two children sometimes created joint chants.

What can we as teachers do to encourage play with language? At least, we can understand how valuable it is, how in a topsy-turvy but profound way, nonsense words can teach about language, even though they are outliers to the system. Perhaps we can find ways to encourage language play, not at the expense of language for communication, but in addition to it. But we must be careful not to intervene so heavily that we limit play's intrinsically joyful quality and thereby its special power.

Encouraging children to write

A classmate of Everett's in the same inner-city classroom in San Diego was a Chicano first-grader, Alberto, who wrote illustrated stories every day on drawing paper at school and paper towels at home, inventing spelling to fit his Spanish accent. The cover of this book shows one of Alberto's drawings and sentences. Here are more examples of Alberto's sentences:

An tis coner is drragn. [In this corner is dragon.]
I like to go to the scwl on the wek. [I like to go to school in the week.]
I like fruwt to et on the morning. [I like fruit to eat in the morning.]
Tis is the syde. [This is the city.]
At tree I see Popy. [At three I see Popeye.]

In Chapter 11, Chomsky explains why children often start out writing this way, and how valuable such creative intellectual work can be. (See Clay 1975, Paul 1976, and Bissex 1980 for more extended discussion of the writing and invented spelling of young children.) Discovering sound-letter relationships through their own attempts to write is much closer to the way children discover the system of their oral language than our usual teaching allows.

References

Bissex, G. L. *Gnys at Wrk: A Child Learns to Read and Write.* Cambridge, Mass.: Harvard University Press, 1980.

Black, R. W. "Crib Talk: Its Role in Language Acquisition." Unpublished doctoral dissertation, Harvard University, 1979.

Cazden, C. B. "Play with Language and Metalinguistic Awareness: One Dimension of Language Experience." In *Dimensions of Language Experience,* ed. C. B. Winsor. New York: Agathon, 1975.

* Cazden, C. B. "Play with Language and Metalinguistic Awareness: One Dimension Teacher—or Does It: A Personal Account." *The Urban Review* 9 (1976): 74-90.

Clay, M. M. *What Did I Write?* Auckland, New Zealand: Heinemann, 1975.

Johnson, H. M. *Children in "The Nursery School."* New York: Agathon, 1972.

Lionni, L. *Inch by Inch.* New York: Obolensky, 1960.

Paul, R. "Invented Spelling in Kindergarten." *Young Children* 31, no. 3 (March 1976): 195-200.

Sartre, J.-P. *The Words.* New York: Fawcett, 1964.

Schickedanz, J. A. " 'Please Read that Story Again!' Exploring Relationships Between Story Reading and Learning to Read." *Young Children* 33, no. 5 (July 1978): 48-55.

Weir, R. H. *Language in the Crib.* The Hague: Mouton, 1962.

Carol Chomsky

11.
Write Now, Read Later

Children ought to learn how to read by creating their own spellings for familiar words as a beginning. This task is not as hard or as exotic as it sounds. Once they know the letters of the alphabet (sounds, not names), they should spend time putting letters together to make words of their own choosing. They can use a set of plastic letters, for example, or alphabet blocks. It is a great thing to put together a word by figuring out for yourself what comes first, what comes next, and so on until you have the whole word laid out in front of you. And what better way to *read* for the first time than to try recognizing the very word you have just carefully built up on the table in front of you?

If the word is to be "born of the creative effort of the learner," as Freire so aptly describes (1970), it cannot be "deposited" in his mind. Children's minds, at four, five, six, are far from linguistic empty space into which reading information is to be poured. What I propose is that children be permitted to be active participants in teaching themselves to read. In fact, they ought to direct the process. By reversing the usual order of read first, write later, this can be allowed to happen.

Children have enormous phonetic acuity and ability to analyze words into their component sounds. Their analyses reflect their own linguistic organization of the phonetic material and do not always coincide with the way adults hear. (Very interesting work is at present being carried out on the linguistic implications of young children's original spelling systems, Read 1971.) Allowed to trust their own ears and their own judgments, many children show amazing facility as they begin to spell. Of course the adult working with them must pay close attention to the way the children pronounce, and expect their spellings to reflect their own pronunciation and linguistic judgments, not the adult's. The product will bear little resemblance to conventional spelling, but no matter. Plenty of time for that later. At this beginning point, the children are busy using information from their own consciousness as to how words sound.

This composing of words according to their sounds (using letter sets, or writing by hand if the child can form letters) is the first step toward read-

---

Reprinted, with permission and additions from *Childhood Education* 47 (1971):296-299.

ing. Once the child has composed a word, he looks at it and tries to recognize it. The recognition is slow, for reading the word seems much harder than writing it. Often the child works it out sound by sound, the reverse of the process by which he wrote it, and then recognition dawns all at once.

If we concede that word recognition, or even just the sounding out of words, appears so much more difficult for children than composing words, why do our reading programs as a matter of course expect children to deal with it first? The natural order is writing first, then reading what you have written. To expect the child to read, as a first step, what someone else has written is backwards, an artificial imposition that denies the child an active role in the whole process. Moreover it takes all the fun out of it. *He* ought to be directing his activities and making the decisions, not you. He ought to pick the words and write them, with your guidance. Or, if you suggest the words, as you will sometimes do, he ought to know that it is up to him to come up with his own spellings.

This whole approach introduces him to the written word by making him aware that it belongs to him and grows out of his own consciousness. He does not begin by viewing it as something alien imposed from without, something arbitrary out there which the adult world has concocted to make life difficult. Rather than a secret that only others are privy to, a ready-made impenetrable code, it becomes for him a means of expressing something in his head. This way the word is, in a very real sense, born of the creative effort of the learner.

How natural it is for very young children to begin spelling on their own was brought home to me again not long ago when a three-year-old of my acquaintance spontaneously began making letter combinations and pronouncing them. (Children can start to do this when they know only a few consonants and vowels. No need at all to wait till they know a great many or all.) My young friend knows by rote how to spell his name and for several months has been able to place plastic letters in a line to spell *H-A-R-R-Y*. As a result of watching "Sesame Street" he knows primarily the names of the letters, although he knows some of their sounds as well.

He sat one day playing with his plastic letters and suddenly said, "Look, it says *Kate*." I turned to look and sure enough he had placed a *KT* in front of him. The magic moment had arrived. Quite impressed with his discovery, he pronounced *Kate* over and over, very distinctly, releasing the *t* loudly. "It sure does," I agreed, marvelling with him at this miracle of the written word. What he was doing was using the *K* according to its name [key], and the *T* according to its sound [tə]. He had worked out for himself a handy combination of the syllabic principle and the alphabetic principle.

He then took an *S* and a *T*, placed them together and said very slowly and distinctly [est]. This too he pronounced over and over, very clearly, with strong *t* release. He then reversed the order to *TS*, and said, "It says *tiss*." He played with the *S* and the *T* for a while, reversing to *ST* [est] and back to *TS* [təss] a number of times, pronouncing correctly each time. The whole process was obviously fascinating to him.

When he left off the ts game, I asked him what word he would like to write now. "Wet," he announced. "OK, what do you need to begin with?" "A [wə]," he answered. "All right, what letter would you use to make [wə]?" "Here's one!" he cried, picking up an *R*.

It is a great thing to put together a word by figuring out for yourself what comes first, what comes next, and so on until you have the whole word laid out in front of you.

Now *R* is correct for him, as a matter of fact. In this child's pronunciation, *R* and *W* are alike when initial in the syllable. For him *wet* begins the same as the second syllable of his name, *Harry,* which he already knew how to spell. He was doing very well indeed to be able to choose it. Furthermore, he had no basis on which to even consider as a possibility the *W* of conventional spelling for writing [wə], since he knows only its name [dʌbəlyu] and not its sound. This illustrates what I mean by the importance of the adult's being attuned to the child's pronunciation and considering what letter names and sounds he has available to express what he says and hears.

Had I said "No!" when Harry chose the *R* and insisted on *W* (which corresponds to no reality for him), he would have gotten that sad message

children so often get in school: "Your judgments are not to be trusted. Do it
my way whether it makes sense or not; forget about reality." Clearly he
can't go through life spelling *wet* with an *R*, and that all gets straightened
out later. What's important at this early stage is that he gets practice in
thinking about how words really sound, gets practice in representing
sounds accurately according to the knowledge of letter names and sounds
he has available *at the time he is writing,* and learns this way that the written
word is for real and not arbitrary. Far better to let him trust his own
accurate judgments and progress according to them than to impose an
arbitrariness that at this point would only interfere.

"OK, now you've got the [wə]. What comes next?" "[eh]," he answered.
"What letter do you need for [eh]?" "This one!" picking up an *A* and
placing it after the *R*. Again, he is right. Think about the names of the
vowels, which is all he knows. *A* is [ey]. If you take off the [y] what you have
left is [e]. A child looking for a way to write [e], choosing from a repertoire
that consists of the vowel names [ey] [iy] [ay] [ow] [yuw], would quite naturally pick [ey].[1] "Good! OK. And then what comes?" "A [tə]," picking up a *T*
and adding it.

And so he has spelled *wet.* To anybody walking into the room at that
moment it looks like *RAT*, but for him and for one who has observed his
construction job, it is clearly *wet*, an entirely accurate rendition of the
word using the means available to him to represent his own phonetic
perceptions.

At this point one might ask a child to read what he has written. I didn't,
in the episode described, because he was tired of the game and his attention
wandered. Several months later (closer to age 3½) he was much better able
to sustain interest and try to read back his carefully composed words.

Two months later, for example, he put together a *T* and an *O*, and said
"tee-oh." These were plastic shapes, from a construction toy, that push
together and stay connected until pulled apart.[2] I asked him what it would
say if the *T* were pronounced [tə], and he looked at it for a while and then
answered "toe." "Do you have anything called that?" I asked. "Yeah," he
replied, "right there," pointing to his foot (an improvement over the last
episode because this time his chance syllable happened to be a real word
and could have its meaning connected to it). I then put together a *DO* for
him (*D* is the only other "letter" shape in the collection), and asked him
what it was: "Dee-oh," he said immediately. "Yes, but suppose the *D* is
pronounced [də]." Again, slowly, "doe." No meaning, for him. He carried
around his *TO* and *DO*, one in each hand, on and off for the rest of the day.

That night he took the box of plastic shapes to bed with him, without his
TO and *DO* which were left downstairs. But the next morning when he

---

[1] This is standard operating procedure in young children's invented spelling systems (see
Read 1971).
[2] It is interesting that this was not an alphabet toy, but a variety of plastic shapes for constructing figures. Some of the pieces happen to look like letters.

called to be taken out of his crib, there on the sheet beside him lay a newly fashioned *TO* and *DO*. He had managed to find more "letters" in the box and put it all together again. The activity was its own reward.

The *TO* and *DO* occupied him only slightly that day, until midafternoon when he came up to me with some excitement, all four letters strung together, *TODO,* and announced, "I made *Toto!*" (pronounced as the dog's name in the *Wizard of Oz*). Well! I shared his excitement, for this was quite a feat, almost too good to be true, and I wondered if it could possibly be meaningful for him. "Do you know anything called that?" I asked, as we both admired his construction. "Yes," he said quietly and almost shyly, "a little dog."

Incidentally, this ability to approach reading through invented spellings is not confined to children of linguists and the like, as is sometimes claimed. Language acquisition, after all, is a creative feat of the first order for which all children show remarkable facility. *All* children are creative when it comes to acquiring their language. There would seem to be little reason to expect, *a priori,* that this additional aspect of language processing, the innovative spelling, should be confined to a select few. The main thing linguists do that other parents perhaps don't is to recognize that children are *able* to spell on their own. They do give their children the idea that they *can,* and they recognize "correctness" taking their cue from the child and a few phonetic perceptions, not from conventional spelling. These seem to be the necessary ingredients.

Montessori (1967) describes what amounts to this same method with lower socioeconomic class children in her Casa dei Bambini in the San Lorenzo quarter of Rome. She went about it in a highly directed manner, to be sure, but the principles are essentially the same and they worked for the San Lorenzo "disadvantaged" children.

> As soon as the child knows some of the vowels and the consonants we place before him the big box containing all the vowels and consonants which he knows. The directress pronounces very clearly a word; for example, "mama," brings out the sound of the *m* very distinctly, repeating the sounds a number of times. Almost always the little one with an impulsive movement seizes an *m* and places it upon the table. The directress repeats "ma-ma." The child selects the *a* and places it near the *m*. He then composes the other syllable very easily. But the reading of the word which he has composed is not so easy. Indeed, he generally succeeds in reading it only after a certain effort. In this case I help the child, urging him to read, and reading the word with him once or twice, always pronouncing very distinctly, *mama, mama.* But once he has understood the mechanism of the game, the child goes forward by himself, and becomes intensely interested. We may pronounce any word, taking care only that the child understands separately the letters of which it is composed. He composes the new word, placing, one after the other, the signs corresponding to the sounds. (Montessori, pp. 282-283)

In a school setting, there is no reason that this approach can't be utilized, if the teacher is interested in having the child "assume from the beginning

the role of creative subject" (Freire 1970). A recent incident in a nursery
school where I was observing illustrates how the spell-it-yourself idea can
be introduced. The children were accustomed to having their drawings
labelled by the teacher, if they wished, and were in the habit of dictating to
her what was to be written. One little boy, aged 3½, had drawn a face. He
came over and asked me to write *man.* "Why don't you write it yourself?" I
asked him. "I don't know how," he replied. "Well," I suggested, "why don't
you figure it out then? What comes first?" *"Man,"* he said quietly, thinking,
and then "[mə]." "OK, what letter would you use to write [mə]?" *"M,"* he
replied, after some thought. "Fine," I said, "let's make an *M.*" Since he
could not yet form letters, I guided his hand and we wrote the *M.* "OK,
what comes next?" Again he pronounced *man* quietly to himself, and said
[nə]." "All right, what letter would you use to write [nə]?" *"N,"* he said.
"OK, let's make the *N.*" When his drawing went up on the wall it was graced
by his own spelling and the closest he could come to his own handwriting.
The omission of the short vowel was natural and correct for this child,
who was just at the very beginning of his spelling career. Several months
later, without instruction, the short vowels began to appear in his spellings.

The particular circumstances of the first writing will of course vary with
each child, depending on his own timing and the situation in which the
need arises. What is constant is the expectation that the child will figure it
out for himself when the time comes.

If a teacher wants to be more purposeful in introducing the spelling idea
and wants to work with a small group of children, this too can be done. One
way is simply to pour three or four sets of plastic letters onto a table top and
start turning them right side up. Whenever I do this in a nursery school,
five or six children immediately come over. Some of them pick the letters
they need and spell out their names. You take it from there. One little girl
put together *Anne,* and we spent some time figuring out how to make other
words by adding different beginnings. I asked her what she would need to
make it say *pan,* and led her step by step through "I need a [pə], *P* is used
for [pə]"; she then found a *P* and put it on. She went through *man, can* and
tan at that sitting and was through for the day. A second child wrote out
Jeremy and then announced that today his name wasn't Jeremy, it was *karate*
(loud sound effects from him at this point). Step by step he put together his
version of *karate: CRIT.* Our conversation went something like this:

What comes first?
A [kə] (he picked a *C* out of the pile)
Then what?
[kərrr . . .] R! (he found an *R* and placed it after the *C*)
Then what?
[kəraaa . . .] (he picked an *I.* This is accurate, since the name of the
letter *I* [ay] contains the sound *ah* as its first part. If the child is looking
for *ah* and working only from letter names, he may quite logically
choose the one in which he hears *ah,* namely the letter *I.*)

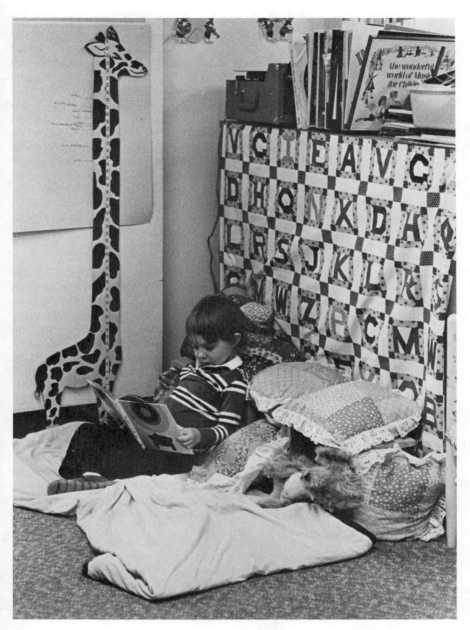

Children ought to be permitted to be active participants in teaching themselves to read. In fact, they ought to direct the process.

He got stuck on the last syallable, so I pronounced the word slowly for him, syllable by syllable, giving the final syllable a *t* pronunciation.[3] At that point he picked the *T* and completed the word.

Along with these suggestions about how to introduce the spelling "artificially," as it were, goes a reminder about the importance of leaving the initiative up to the child. True, the child somehow has to get the idea that he can spell, and to this end the above descriptions suggest several avenues of approach. But it's most important that the activity develop as an expressive one, and not degenerate into a form of exercise. Whatever means the teacher uses to introduce the notion, her function should be to give the child access to the spelling, not to require it of him. How much writing he will eventually produce, if any, depends on his own inclination and interest.

An analogy to painting and drawing may be useful here. In painting, the teacher makes paper and paints available and may encourage the child to go ahead and use them, but she is prepared to leave the decisions of when, how and what pretty much up to him. Her view of the function of children's art precludes prescriptions and requirements. The early spelling ought to be treated in much the same way.

If the teacher encourages the writing once it begins to appear, if she welcomes and values the spellings and transmits to the child her feeling that he is doing something exciting and worthwhile, some children are likely to go ahead. If the teacher can interpret the spellings more fluently by having some prior knowledge of what to expect, so much the better. It might help her to be aware of various features that appear at different stages in the child's progress: e.g., that certain vowels will be omitted (*DG-dog, FRN-fern*), that preconsonantal *M* and *N* will be left out (*WOT-won't*), that short vowels will be altered systematically (*MEKS-mix, WAT-wet*), that *TR* and *DR* will be written *CHR* and *JR* (*CHRAN-train, JRAGIN-dragon*), and so on. But even without specific background, the sympathetic teacher can welcome the spellings and place a high value on them. Most important is that the child comes to trust his own linguistic perceptions, understands that he has a viable means of expressing them, and gets plenty of practice doing so.

For those children whose phonetic awareness doesn't yet permit this kind of word composition, the thing to do is to work on developing the awareness. Let them get to the point where they can make their own productions before they are expected to read other people's productions. This would be true preparation for learning to read!

If the child writes first, the written word grows out of his own consciousness and belongs to him. Why not let him? Let him trust his linguistic judgments, and expect of him only that he accurately express his own perceptions using the means available to him. With this background and familiarity, conventional spelling poses no problem when he comes to it gradually later on. If anything, learning to read seems to be considerably

---

[3] This is questionable procedure, but he was stuck. It was, after all, his first try. He should have done the pronouncing himself, and later on, with more experience, he ought to be able to.

facilitated for the spontaneous speller. In many cases, he quite simply *teaches himself when he is ready.*

Typically, the speller reaches a point where he begins to ask about words that he sees around him. Either he attempts to pronounce them, reading them off phonetically in order to identify them, or he asks what they say. When this time comes, such a child seems suddenly to notice all the print in the world around him—street signs, food labels, newspaper headlines, printing on cartons, books, billboards, everything. He tries to read everything, already having a good foundation in translating from pronunciation to print. If help is provided when he asks for it, he makes out wonderfully well. It is a tremendously exciting time for him.

I think that what helps the child most of all at this point is his heightened activity level. Learning to read, or at first to identify printed words, surely involves forming hypotheses about the relations (direct and indirect) of conventional spelling to pronunciation, changing these hypotheses as new evidence is added and eventually arriving at a system of interpretation that is in accord with the facts. This hypothesis construction is an active process, taking the child far beyond the "rules" that can be offered him by the best of patterned, programmed or linguistic approaches. The more the child is prepared to do for himself, the better off he is.

This ease in learning to read after experience with invented spellings is very much in line with Piaget's view that "children have real understanding only of that which they invent themselves, and each time we try to teach them something too quickly, we keep them from reinventing it themselves" (in Silberman 1970). The printed word "belongs" to the spontaneous speller in a way in which it cannot, at least at the start, belong to children who have experienced it only ready-made.

References

Freire, P. "The Adult Literacy Process as Cultural Action for Freedom." *Harvard Educational Review* 40, no. 2 (May 1970): 208.

Montessori, M. *The Montessori Method.* Cambridge, Mass.: Robert Bentley, 1967. Reprinted with permission.

Read, C. "Pre-School Children's Knowledge of English Phonology." *Harvard Educational Review* 41, no. 1 (February 1971): 1-34.

Silberman, C. *Crisis in the Classroom.* New York: Random House, 1970.

Part IV
Evaluation

Courtney B. Cazden

12.
On Evaluation

Planning evaluations and choosing objectives are clearly similar tasks. In order to plan any evaluation, it is necessary to outline what one is trying to accomplish. Once objectives are established, it is easy to decide what should be observed or listened to and how, to determine if progress is being made. We should look for evidence of progress both in individual children and in the program as a whole.

Progress in individual children

For assessing the progress of individual children, published tests have limited usefulness. First, many are designed for group administration, and group tests are simply inappropriate for young children. To take a test in a group, children have to keep up with the group pace, wait when necessary without making extra marks, and then attend to the right place on demand. One can never be sure whether a child's wrong answer is due to the lack of such test-taking skills, or to lack of knowledge the test is supposed to assess. Ambron (1978) reported on the problems an experienced teacher had in administering CIRCUS (Educational Testing Service 1974) to small groups of preschool children. Her findings would apply to all group paper-and-pencil tests:

> First, even with practice items, children could not follow the directions. They could not find the correct page nor mark the appropriate items, even when they knew the right answer because it had been shouted out. (Ambron 1978, p. 20)

Second, most standardized tests are designed to yield scores which indicate whether one child is better, in some sense, than another, and to rank them accordingly. They are not designed to show specifically what a child does or does not know, can or cannot do. In technical terms, most tests are norm-referenced, whereas teachers need criterion-referenced measures to give information about which children have or have not achieved particular objectives.

For example, standardized vocabulary tests, such as the Peabody Picture Vocabulary Test (American Guidance Service 1965), pick a small and sup-

Teachers will get better diagnostic information on individual children, and more useful information on the success of their program, by conducting informal checks themselves than by arranging for the administration of standardized tests.

posedly representative set of the universe of words. When children are tested for their knowledge of these words, the result is a rank ordering of children, or an assignment of a mental-age equivalent, according to the number of words whose meanings they know. The particular words used in the test are not important in themselves; they are merely supposed to be indicators of more general knowledge. But testing children's knowledge of particular words that a program or teacher has decided to teach would be much more useful. See Bartlett's discussion in Chapter 4 of the evaluation suggestions that accompany particular language curricula.

Teachers will get better diagnostic information on individual children, and more useful information on the success of their program, by conducting informal checks themselves than by arranging for the administration of standardized tests. Frequently, teaching situations can also double as evaluation situations. For example, many aspects of language can be both taught and assessed while children play Language Lotto (Appleton-Century-Crofts 1966). There are six boxes in the set: *Objects, Actions, More Actions, Prepositions, Compound Sentences,* and *Relationships.* Each set can be played at three levels, depending on the complexity of the child's task. The child visually matches a card to the one held by the teacher; the child locates the correct picture from the teacher's verbal description; finally, the child can supply the description. A checklist is provided (or could be easily constructed) so that a teacher or aide can keep track of which level of which particular box each child can play. The two-person communication game described by Gleason in Chapter 5 can also be used both to teach and to assess.

Usually, some combination of more structured situations which could be called tests and sensitive listening to children's ongoing observations are needed, because not all behaviors appear spontaneously, even if they have been learned. Furthermore, even if certain behaviors are present, the natural situation is often not sufficiently controlled so that inferences about progress can be made. For example, if one child's speech is hard to understand, the teacher needs to know if the child is becoming more intelligible as the months go by. It is not sufficient to know that the teacher, or the child's classmates, can understand the child better; that could be a result of their increasing familiarity with the child rather than any objective change in speech. To check further, the teacher (or aide) could record samples of the child's conversation—maybe retelling a story—at the beginning, middle, and end of the school year and then play the tape to people who do not know the child—other parents, other staff, visitors, etc. Do they understand an increasing proportion of the speech?

Of all aspects of human behavior, speech is probably the most susceptible to subtle situational influences. This is especially true of the influences inherent in any testing situation. This is also the case for subjects who are at any social disadvantage vis-á-vis the tester—e.g., child to adult, minority group member to majority group member, or outsider to formal bureaucratic institution. For this reason, it is essential to include observations of children in situations natural in their own culture in any complete evaluation plan. See Cazden (1971) and Tough (1976) for many detailed suggestions.

Progress in the program

As we discussed in Part I, any group setting for young children—in contrast to conversation in the home—requires special planning. Children's progress in language development will depend on qualities of the program environment; thus it is essential for a program staff to do periodic formative evaluations of that environment that can be used to reform and improve the program itself.

Consider one possible program goal related to learning to read: to interest children in books and encourage parents to borrow books to read to their children at home. Answers to these questions will help staff determine how well their goal is being met: During free-choice periods, how many children go to the library corner and look at books by themselves? How many requests do adults get to "read to me" during a day? How many children listen attentively during story time? How many books have been borrowed by parents during the week? Which books have become special favorites, as shown by signs of extra wear? If observations were made to answer these questions in October, December, and February, were there any trends during the school year?

With such information, the staff could discuss what could be changed to encourage even more book reading at school and at home.

See Mattick and Perkins (1978) for extensive suggestions for evaluating the learning environment.

References

Ambron, S. R. "Review of CIRCUS." In *The Eighth Mental Measurements Yearbook*, ed. O. K. Buros. Highland Park, N.J.: Gryphon Press, 1978.

American Guidance Service. *Peabody Picture Vocabulary Test*. Circle Pines, Minn.: American Guidance Service, 1965.

Appleton-Century-Crofts. *Language Lotto*. New York: Appleton-Century-Crofts, 1966.

Cazden, C. B. "Evaluating Language Learning in Early Childhood Education." In *On Formative and Summative Evaluation of Student Learning*, eds. B. S. Bloom, T. Hastings, and G. Madaus. New York: McGraw-Hill, 1971.

Educational Testing Service. *CIRCUS*. Princeton, N.J.: Educational Testing Service, 1974.

Mattick, I., and Perkins, F. J. *Guidelines for Observation and Assessment: An Approach to Evaluating the Learning Environment of a Day Care Center*. Revised ed. Washington, D.C.: Day Care and Child Development Council, 1978.

* Tough, J. *Listening to Children Talking*. London: Ward Lock Educational Publishing, 1976.

Appendix A

Annotated Bibliography

The following is a very selective list of books about language in early childhood education for teachers of young children.

Ashton-Warner, S. *Spinster.* New York: Bantam, 1961.
  A fictional version of *Teacher.* Includes a rich account of using children's own words for teaching beginning reading in New Zealand.
Ashton-Warner, S. *Teacher.* New York: Simon & Schuster, 1963.
  The ideas of *Spinster* but without the Maori children.
Blank, M. *Teaching Learning in the Preschool: A Dialogue Approach.* Columbus, Ohio: Merrill, 1973.
  The theory and practice of teacher-child interactions for cognitive development.
Cazden, C. B. *Child Language and Education.* New York: Holt, Rinehart & Winston, 1972.
  The most complete account of the author's ideas on child language.
Cazden, C. B. "Play with Language and Metalinguistic Awareness: One Dimension of Language Experience." In *Dimensions of Language Experience,* ed. C. B. Winsor. New York: Agathon, 1975. Also in *Urban Review* 9 (1976): 74-90.
  Discussion of the cognitive value of language play.
Chukovsky, K. *From Two to Five.* Berkeley: University of California Press, 1963.
  A delightful book about children's language and language in books for children by a Soviet author.
deVilliers, P. A., and deVilliers, J. G. *Early Language.* Cambridge, Mass.: Harvard University Press, 1979.
  Excellent and readable overview of language development.
Hawkins, F. P. *The Logic of Action: Young Children at Work.* New York: Pantheon, 1973.
  A nursery school teacher's account of "the language of action" in science experiences with six deaf children.
Johnson, J., and Tamburrini, J. *Informal Reading and Writing.* New York: Citation Press, 1972.
  Part of a series on infant schools written by British experts.
Lindfors, J. W. *Children's Language and Learning.* Englewood Cliffs, N.J.: Prentice-Hall, 1980.
  Excellent general text for teachers.
Luria, A. R., and Yudovich, F. *Speech and the Development of Mental Processes in the Child.* New York: Penguin Books, 1971.
  Account of a Soviet experiment on the language education of twins.
McAfee, O. "The Right Words." *Young Children* 23, no. 2 (November 1967): 74-78.
  Still sound advice on teacher language.

Moffett, J., and Wagner, B. J. *Student-Centered Language Arts and Reading: A Handbook for Teachers.* Boston: Houghton Mifflin, 1976.
   The school language arts program which best carries out the implications of what we know about language development.
Paley, V. *Wally's Stories.* Cambridge, Mass.: Harvard University Press, 1980.
   A kindergarten teacher's report on her use of stories in dramatizations.
Paley, V. *White Teacher.* Cambridge, Mass.: Harvard University Press, 1979.
   A kindergarten teacher's account of how her Black children helped her to face herself.
Richardson, E. S. *In the Early World.* New York: Pantheon, 1964.
   A beautiful book on informal education in New Zealand. Includes rich accounts of children's writings and all other forms of creative expression.
Spradley, T. S., and Spradley, J. P. *Deaf Like Me.* New York: Random House, 1978.
   The story of a profoundly deaf child, by her father and his anthropologist brother, that is a powerful plea for sign language.
Tough, J. *Listening to Children Talking: A Guide to the Appraisal of Children's Use of Language.* London: Ward Lock Educational, 1976.
   Many suggestions for assessing children's language.
Tough, J. *Talking and Learning: A Guide to Fostering Communication Skills in Nursery and Infant Schools.* London: Ward Lock Educational, 1977.
   Many excellent ideas for teaching.
Weber, L. *The English Infant School of Informal Education.* Englewood Cliffs, N.J.: Prentice-Hall, 1971.
   Includes a thoughtful discussion of language practices.
Weeks, T. E. *Born to Talk.* Rowley, Mass.: Newbury House, 1979.
   Excellent and readable overview of language development.
Whiteman, M. F. *Reactions to Ann Arbor: Vernacular Black English and Education.* Washington, D.C.: Center for Applied Linguistics, 1980.
   A state-of-the-art review of the role of nonstandard dialect in education.

Index

Information About NAEYC

NAEYC is. . .

. . . a membership-supported organization of people committed to fostering the growth and development of children from birth through age 8. Membership is open to all who share a desire to serve and act on behalf of the needs and rights of young children.

NAEYC provides. . .

. . . educational services and resources to adults who work with and for children, including

- **Young Children,** *the* journal for early childhood educators
- **Books, posters, brochures, and videos** to expand your knowledge and commitment to young children, with topics including infants, curriculum, research, discipline, teacher education, and parent involvement
- An **Annual Conference** that brings people from all over the country to share their expertise and advocate on behalf of children and families
- **Week of the Young Child** celebrations sponsored by NAEYC Affiliate Groups across the nation to call public attention to the needs and rights of children and families
- **Insurance plans** for individuals and programs
- **Public affairs information** for knowledgeable advocacy efforts at all levels of government and through the media
- **The National Academy of Early Childhood Programs,** a voluntary accreditation system for high-quality programs for children
- The **Information Service,** a computer-based, centralized source of information sharing, distribution, and collaboration.

For free information about membership, publications, or other NAEYC services. . .

. . .call NAEYC at 202-232-8777 or 800-424-2460 or write to NAEYC, 1834 Connecticut Ave., NW, Washington, DC 20009-5786.

9/
LH